# Time-Saver Details for Store Planning and Design

# Time-Saver Details for Store Planning and Design

Charles E. Broudy, FAIA

Vilma Barr

**McGraw-Hill, Inc.**
New York   San Francisco   Washington, D.C.   Auckland   Bogotá
Caracas   Lisbon   London   Madrid   Mexico City   Milan
Montreal   New Delhi   San Juan   Singapore
Sydney   Tokyo   Toronto

Library of Congress Cataloging-in-Publication Data

Broudy, Charles E.
    Time-saver details for store planning and design / Charles E.
Broudy, Vilma Barr.
        p.      cm.
    Includes index.
    ISBN 0-07-004386-8
    1. Stores, Retail—Planning.   2. Stores, Retail—Design and
construction.   I. Barr, Vilma.   II. Title.
HF5429.B667      1995
658.2'3—dc20                                            94-37718
                                                           CIP

1 2 3 4 5 6 7 8 9 0   KGP/KGP   9 0 9 8 7 6 5 4


ISBN 0-07-004386-8


*The sponsoring editor for this book was Joel Stein, the editing supervisor was
Stephen M. Smith, and the production supervisor was Suzanne W. B. Rapcavage.
It was set in Garamond Light by McGraw-Hill's Professional Book Group
composition unit.*

*Printed and bound by Arcata Graphics/Kingsport.*


This book is printed on acid-free paper.


INTERNATIONAL EDITION

*To the clients of Charles E. Broudy & Associates, and to the staff members of the firm whose talents have helped to produce this book.*

# Contents

# Introduction

*Time-Saver Details for Store Planning and Design* is a companion book to the Second Edition of our *Designing to Sell: A Complete Guide to Retail Store Planning and Design,* published by McGraw-Hill in 1990. Together, the two books form a set of basic references on the topic of designing for retail facilities for use by architects, interior designers, manufacturers, and contractors.

From more than 30 years in the specialty architectural practice in store design of Charles E. Broudy & Associates, we have culled this collection of ideas for store interiors and fixtures. Included in this book's 20 chapters are drawings that represent architectural and display elements that were created by CEB&A, and other elements that are basic to the field and modified to apply to a variety of merchandising situations. Each chapter has examples to help develop solutions that employ elements that are functional, are appealing, and enhance the perceived value of the merchandise carried in the store.

"Point-of-view" in merchandising parlance stands for the retailer's differentiation strategy for product selection and target market approach. By understanding the merchant's point-of-view, a distinctive design will integrate the interior into a unified selling environment.

## Tips and Guidelines for Using *Time-Saver Details for Store Planning and Design*

- *20 Chapters.* This book is divided into 20 chapters organized by store type. Retailing thrives on change, so we expect that new store types will be emerging in coming years. As merchants mind the market and fine-tune their organization's differentiation strategy, they will no doubt invent new retail establishments with targeted consumer appeal. The drawings presented in *Time-Saver Details for Store Planning and Design* can be used as a "kit of parts." Once you become familiar with the sequence of the drawings, you will be able to mix and match components and concepts for a flexible design approach that will be new, fresh, and enticing.

- *Chapter Opening Page.* Each chapter begins with a floor plan relating to the chapter's store type.

- *Chapter Second Page.* The second page of each chapter contains a photo of a recent project that demonstrates how the drawings in the chapter can be translated into three dimensions to create an integrated, sales-stimulating retail environment. On this page also appears "Tips and Guidelines," which highlights specific planning and programming aspects of the store type as well as specialized customer requirements.

- *Chapter Drawings.* The drawings that are found on subsequent pages of each chapter are intended to be used as a base or springboard for creating innovative fixturing and detailing. Not all dimensions are indicated, as they would be in a set of working drawings. The drawings in this book can be applied in their present form or modified and adapted for size, finish, and components.


Fast turn-around, flexibility, and tight project control characterize the demands inherent in the design and construction of retail stores. Certainly, computerization has changed the way we communicate verbally and with images. High-tech tools such as computer-aided design and drafting (CADD), scanners, and high-speed printers have introduced new dimensions into the process of bringing a store to life. Accurate prioritizing of merchant needs and customer requirements, and successful project management still depend on informed decision-making by the professionals who turn store design ideas into reality. Our intention for *Time-Saver Details for Store Planning and Design* is that it becomes a standard handbook and creative asset for the industry.

*Charles E. Broudy, FAIA*
*Vilma Barr, ASID (Press)*

# Acknowledgments

The authors would like to express their sincere appreciation to David Schwing, Michael Broudy, Kirk Fromm, and other staff members of Charles E. Broudy & Associates for their cooperation and extraordinary efforts to carry out their demanding assignments and maintain the highest standards of esthetics and quality.

At McGraw-Hill, we would like to thank Joel Stein, Senior Editor, and Tom Kowalczyk, Senior Production Manager, for encouraging and guiding us in the technical process of preparing the drawings to meet new electronic standards for printing.

# Time-Saver Details for Store Planning and Design

# Women's Apparel Stores

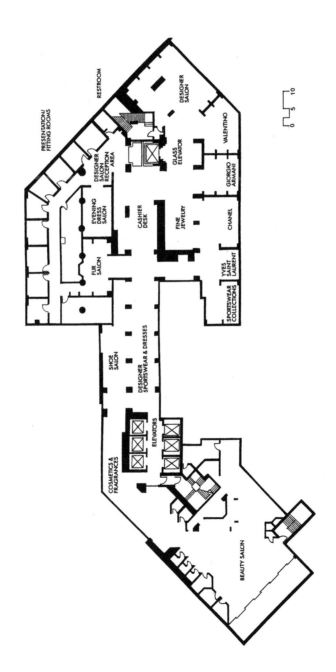

Labels in the floor plan:
- PRESENTATION/ FITTING ROOMS
- RESTROOM
- DESIGNER SALON
- DESIGNER SALON RECEPTION AREA
- GLASS ELEVATOR
- VALENTINO
- EVENING DRESS SALON
- CASHIER DESK
- FINE JEWELRY
- GIORGIO ARMANI
- FUR SALON
- CHANEL
- YVES SAINT LAURENT
- SPORTSWEAR COLLECTIONS
- SHOE SALON
- DESIGNER SPORTSWEAR & DRESSES
- COSMETICS & FRAGRANCES
- ELEVATORS
- BEAUTY SALON

0 5 10

**UPSCALE WOMEN'S APPAREL STORE ON THE THIRD FLOOR OF A MULTI-USE BUILDING IN A DOWNTOWN URBAN LOCATION**

## Tips and Guidelines

1. Interior environment should reflect targeted demographics: low-, mid-, and high-end, and price points.

2. Store's design should reflect the merchandise categories carried: career, active sportswear, juniors, salon.

3. Store's layout should lead the customer around the selling floor so that all areas are shopped.

   - Americans with Disabilities Act (ADA) requires that aisles be at least three feet wide to allow for a wheelchair.

4. Consider both built-in and movable elements for merchandise display.

5. Power and lighting should be planned for both in-store merchandise and human needs, and for visual merchandiser's requirements for display windows.

   - Determine open or closed back for windows early in programming.

6. Placement and style of interior and exterior signs should be integrated into overall design concept.

7. Location and configuration of cashwrap station are pivotal planning decisions. Consider:

   - Bag and box storage.
   - Wrapping and writing surfaces.
   - Surveillance position.

8. Fitting rooms should support the store's image. Consider:

   - Privacy.
   - Lighting.
   - Security.

9. Provide for a seating area where persons accompanying the shopper can wait comfortably.

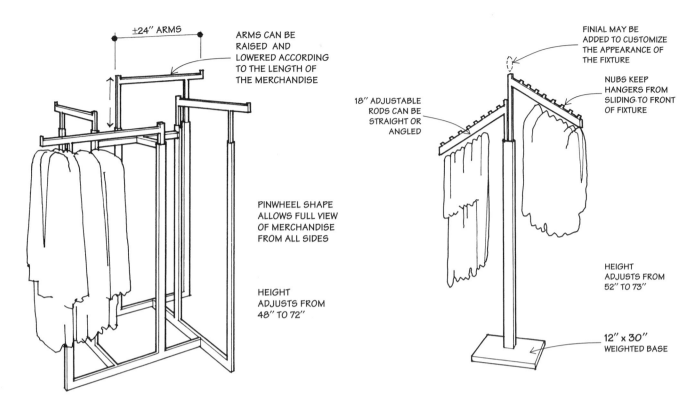

±24" ARMS

ARMS CAN BE RAISED AND LOWERED ACCORDING TO THE LENGTH OF THE MERCHANDISE

PINWHEEL SHAPE ALLOWS FULL VIEW OF MERCHANDISE FROM ALL SIDES

HEIGHT ADJUSTS FROM 48" TO 72"

FINIAL MAY BE ADDED TO CUSTOMIZE THE APPEARANCE OF THE FIXTURE

NUBS KEEP HANGERS FROM SLIDING TO FRONT OF FIXTURE

18" ADJUSTABLE RODS CAN BE STRAIGHT OR ANGLED

HEIGHT ADJUSTS FROM 52" TO 73"

12" x 30" WEIGHTED BASE

**FOUR-WAY HANG FIXTURE**          **T-STAND**

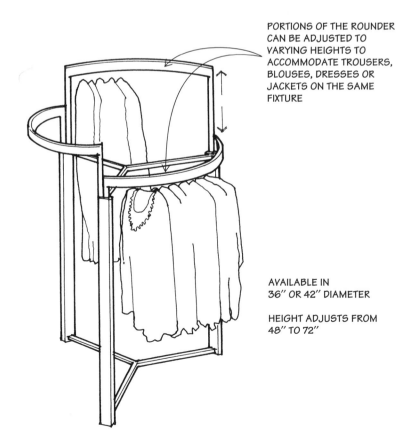

PORTIONS OF THE ROUNDER CAN BE ADJUSTED TO VARYING HEIGHTS TO ACCOMMODATE TROUSERS, BLOUSES, DRESSES OR JACKETS ON THE SAME FIXTURE

AVAILABLE IN 36" OR 42" DIAMETER

HEIGHT ADJUSTS FROM 48" TO 72"

**SPLIT ROUNDER RACKS**

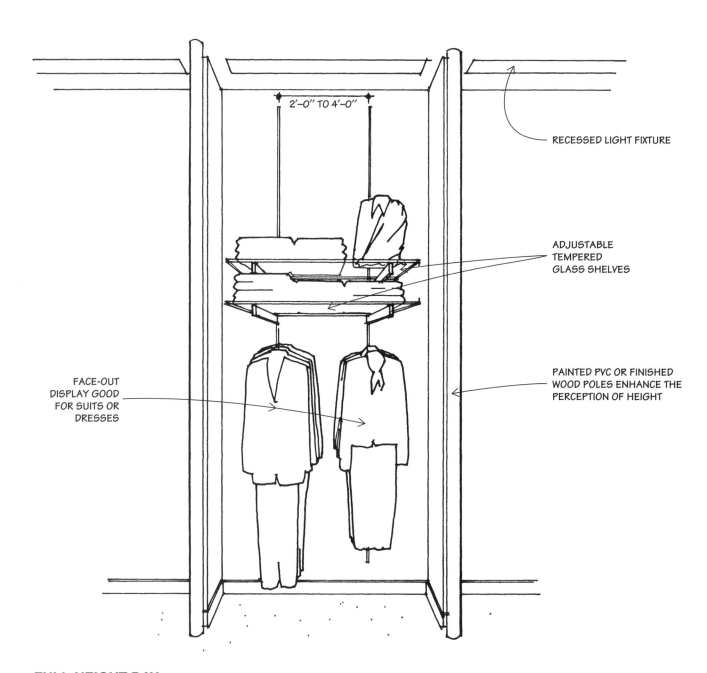

2'-0" TO 4'-0"

RECESSED LIGHT FIXTURE

ADJUSTABLE
TEMPERED
GLASS SHELVES

FACE-OUT
DISPLAY GOOD
FOR SUITS OR
DRESSES

PAINTED PVC OR FINISHED
WOOD POLES ENHANCE THE
PERCEPTION OF HEIGHT

**FULL-HEIGHT BAY**

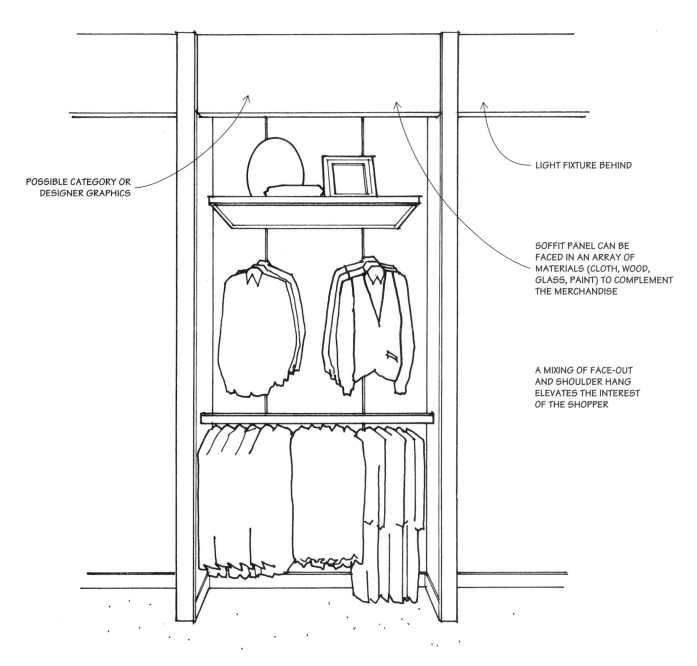

POSSIBLE CATEGORY OR
DESIGNER GRAPHICS

LIGHT FIXTURE BEHIND

SOFFIT PANEL CAN BE
FACED IN AN ARRAY OF
MATERIALS (CLOTH, WOOD,
GLASS, PAINT) TO COMPLEMENT
THE MERCHANDISE

A MIXING OF FACE-OUT
AND SHOULDER HANG
ELEVATES THE INTEREST
OF THE SHOPPER

**BAY WITH VALANCE**

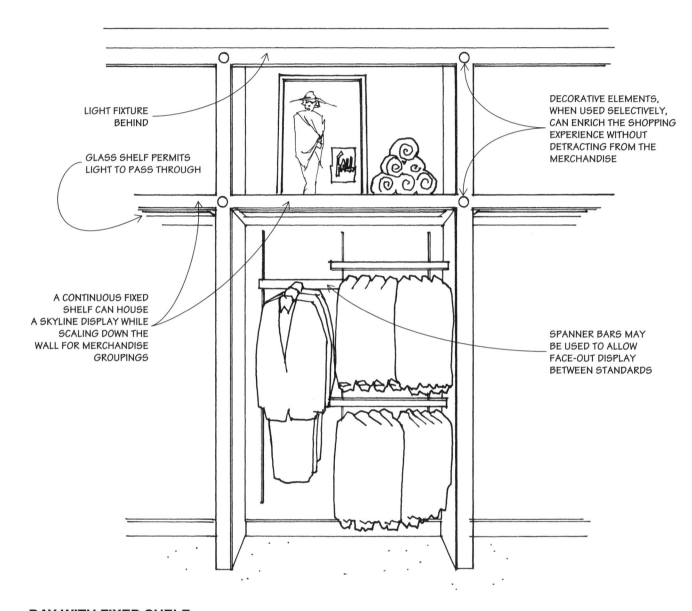

LIGHT FIXTURE
BEHIND

GLASS SHELF PERMITS
LIGHT TO PASS THROUGH

DECORATIVE ELEMENTS,
WHEN USED SELECTIVELY,
CAN ENRICH THE SHOPPING
EXPERIENCE WITHOUT
DETRACTING FROM THE
MERCHANDISE

A CONTINUOUS FIXED
SHELF CAN HOUSE
A SKYLINE DISPLAY WHILE
SCALING DOWN THE
WALL FOR MERCHANDISE
GROUPINGS

SPANNER BARS MAY
BE USED TO ALLOW
FACE-OUT DISPLAY
BETWEEN STANDARDS

**BAY WITH FIXED SHELF**

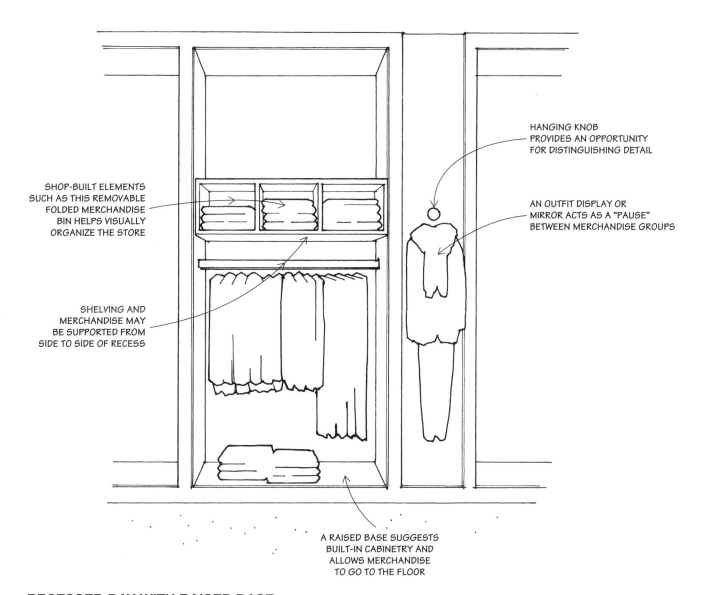

HANGING KNOB
PROVIDES AN OPPORTUNITY
FOR DISTINGUISHING DETAIL

AN OUTFIT DISPLAY OR
MIRROR ACTS AS A "PAUSE"
BETWEEN MERCHANDISE GROUPS

SHOP-BUILT ELEMENTS
SUCH AS THIS REMOVABLE
FOLDED MERCHANDISE
BIN HELPS VISUALLY
ORGANIZE THE STORE

SHELVING AND
MERCHANDISE MAY
BE SUPPORTED FROM
SIDE TO SIDE OF RECESS

A RAISED BASE SUGGESTS
BUILT-IN CABINETRY AND
ALLOWS MERCHANDISE
TO GO TO THE FLOOR

**RECESSED BAY WITH RAISED BASE**

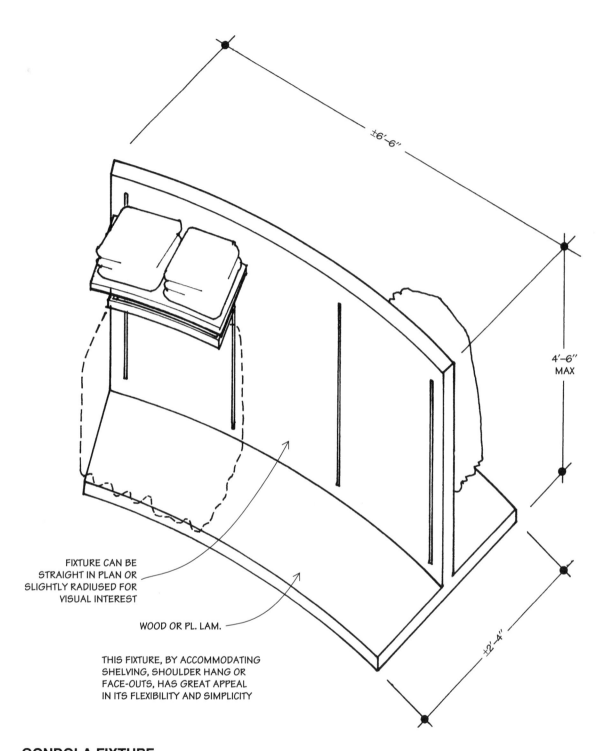

±6'-6"

4'-6"
MAX

FIXTURE CAN BE
STRAIGHT IN PLAN OR
SLIGHTLY RADIUSED FOR
VISUAL INTEREST

WOOD OR PL. LAM.

THIS FIXTURE, BY ACCOMMODATING
SHELVING, SHOULDER HANG OR
FACE-OUTS, HAS GREAT APPEAL
IN ITS FLEXIBILITY AND SIMPLICITY

±2'-4"

## GONDOLA FIXTURE

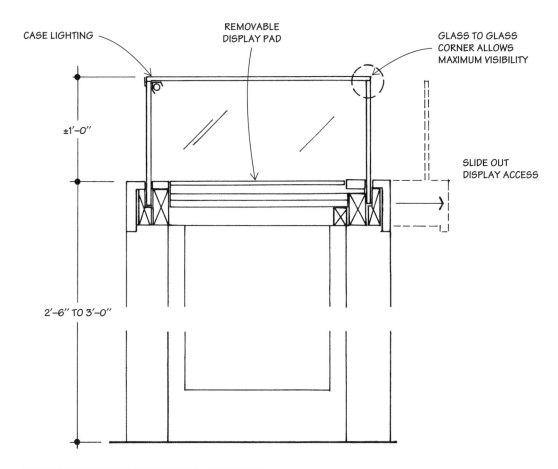

CASE LIGHTING

REMOVABLE
DISPLAY PAD

GLASS TO GLASS
CORNER ALLOWS
MAXIMUM VISIBILITY

±1'-0"

SLIDE OUT
DISPLAY ACCESS

2'-6" TO 3'-0"

## SECTION THROUGH DISPLAY CASE

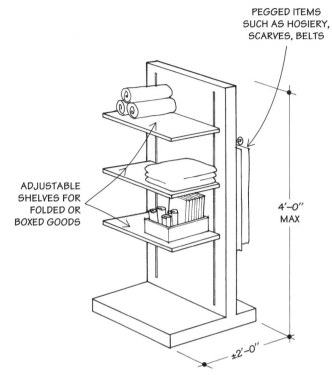

PEGGED ITEMS
SUCH AS HOSIERY,
SCARVES, BELTS

ADJUSTABLE
SHELVES FOR
FOLDED OR
BOXED GOODS

4'-0"
MAX

±2'-0"

**ACCESSORY FIXTURE**

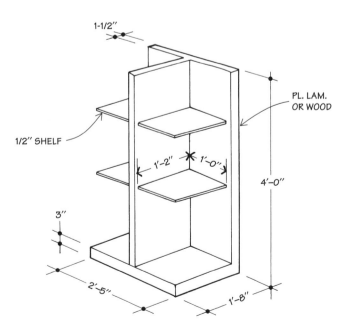

1-1/2"

PL. LAM.
OR WOOD

1/2" SHELF

1'-2"    1'-0"

4'-0"

3"

2'-5"    1'-8"

**DISPLAY UNIT**

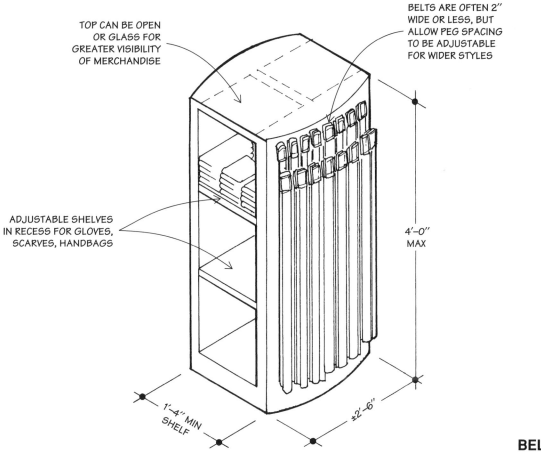

TOP CAN BE OPEN
OR GLASS FOR
GREATER VISIBILITY
OF MERCHANDISE

BELTS ARE OFTEN 2"
WIDE OR LESS, BUT
ALLOW PEG SPACING
TO BE ADJUSTABLE
FOR WIDER STYLES

ADJUSTABLE SHELVES
IN RECESS FOR GLOVES,
SCARVES, HANDBAGS

4'-0"
MAX

1'-4" MIN
SHELF

±2'-6"

**BELT FIXTURE**

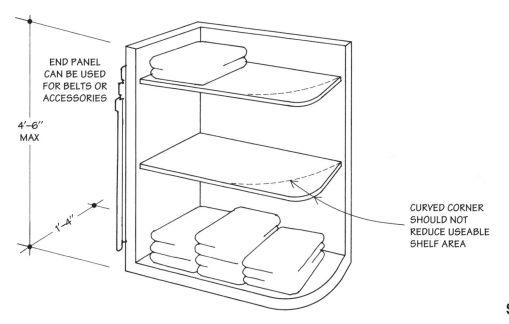

END PANEL
CAN BE USED
FOR BELTS OR
ACCESSORIES

4'-6"
MAX

1'-4"

CURVED CORNER
SHOULD NOT
REDUCE USEABLE
SHELF AREA

**SHELVED FIXTURE**

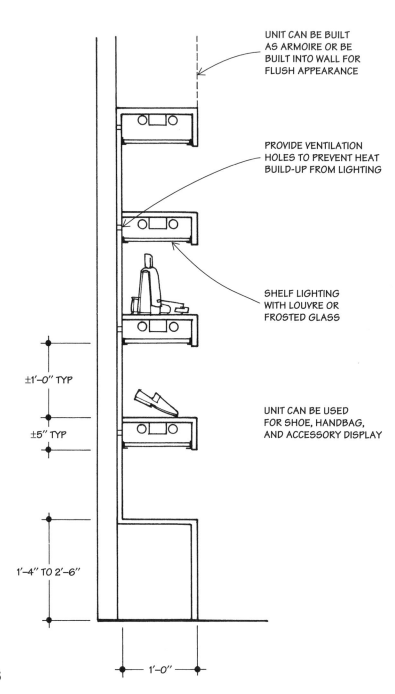

UNIT CAN BE BUILT
AS ARMOIRE OR BE
BUILT INTO WALL FOR
FLUSH APPEARANCE

PROVIDE VENTILATION
HOLES TO PREVENT HEAT
BUILD-UP FROM LIGHTING

SHELF LIGHTING
WITH LOUVRE OR
FROSTED GLASS

UNIT CAN BE USED
FOR SHOE, HANDBAG,
AND ACCESSORY DISPLAY

±1'–0" TYP

±5" TYP

1'–4" TO 2'–6"

1'–0"

**SECTION THROUGH DISPLAY RECESS**

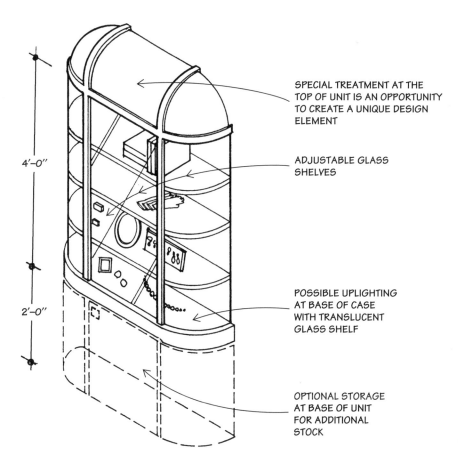

SPECIAL TREATMENT AT THE
TOP OF UNIT IS AN OPPORTUNITY
TO CREATE A UNIQUE DESIGN
ELEMENT

ADJUSTABLE GLASS
SHELVES

POSSIBLE UPLIGHTING
AT BASE OF CASE
WITH TRANSLUCENT
GLASS SHELF

OPTIONAL STORAGE
AT BASE OF UNIT
FOR ADDITIONAL
STOCK

4'-0"

2'-0"

**VITRINE**

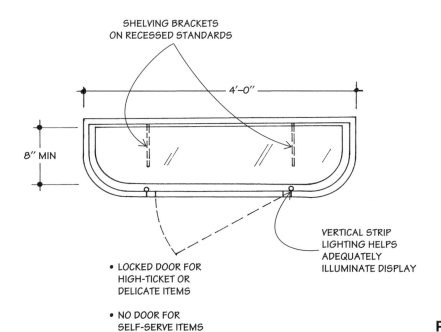

SHELVING BRACKETS
ON RECESSED STANDARDS

4'-0"

8" MIN

VERTICAL STRIP
LIGHTING HELPS
ADEQUATELY
ILLUMINATE DISPLAY

• LOCKED DOOR FOR
HIGH-TICKET OR
DELICATE ITEMS

• NO DOOR FOR
SELF-SERVE ITEMS

**PLAN OF VITRINE**

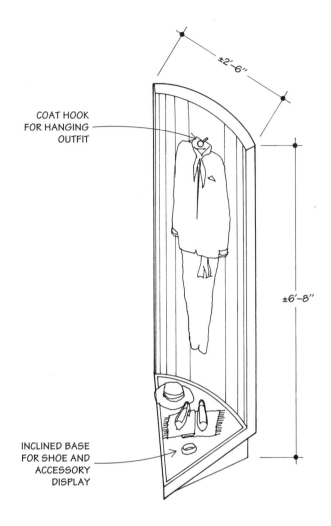

±2'–6"

COAT HOOK
FOR HANGING
OUTFIT

±6'–8"

INCLINED BASE
FOR SHOE AND
ACCESSORY
DISPLAY

**HIGH WINDOW DISPLAY**

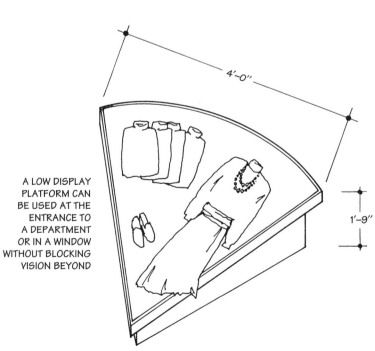

4'–0"

A LOW DISPLAY
PLATFORM CAN
BE USED AT THE
ENTRANCE TO
A DEPARTMENT
OR IN A WINDOW
WITHOUT BLOCKING
VISION BEYOND

1'–9"

**LOW WINDOW DISPLAY**

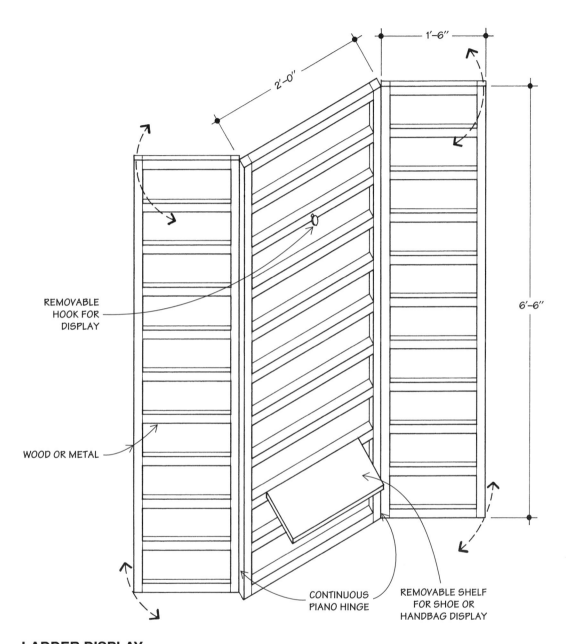

2'-0"

1'-6"

6'-6"

REMOVABLE
HOOK FOR
DISPLAY

WOOD OR METAL

CONTINUOUS
PIANO HINGE

REMOVABLE SHELF
FOR SHOE OR
HANDBAG DISPLAY

**LADDER DISPLAY**

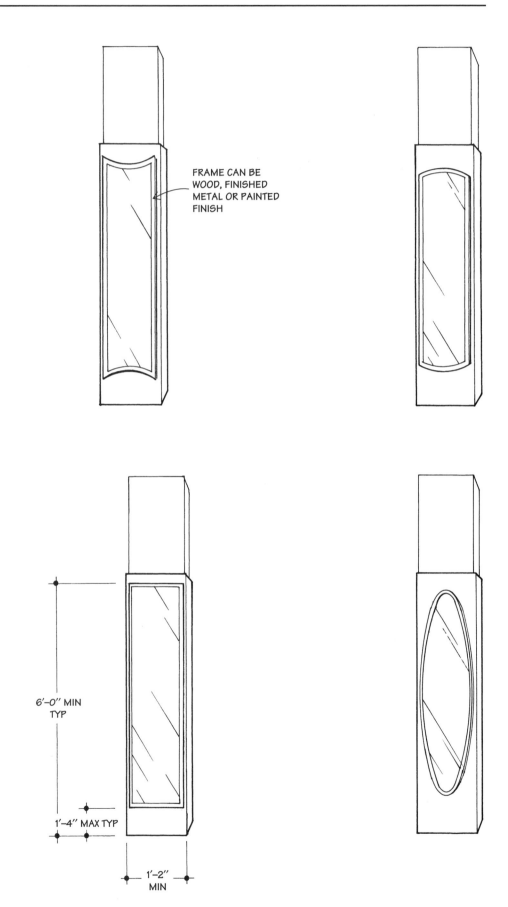

FRAME CAN BE
WOOD, FINISHED
METAL OR PAINTED
FINISH

6'-0'' MIN
TYP

1'-4'' MAX TYP

1'-2''
MIN

**VARIOUS SHAPES FOR COLUMN-MOUNTED MIRRORS**

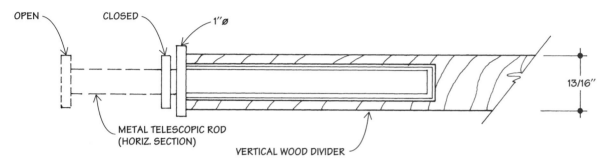

OPEN

CLOSED

1"Ø

13/16"

METAL TELESCOPIC ROD
(HORIZ. SECTION)

VERTICAL WOOD DIVIDER

## PLAN

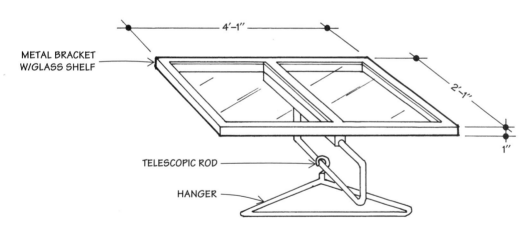

METAL BRACKET
W/GLASS SHELF

4'–1"

2'–1"

1"

TELESCOPIC ROD

HANGER

## HANG ROD WITH SHELF

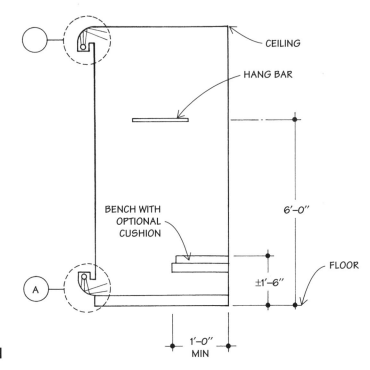

CEILING

HANG BAR

BENCH WITH
OPTIONAL
CUSHION

6'-0"

FLOOR

±1'-6"

A

1'-0"
MIN

**FITTING ROOM SECTION**

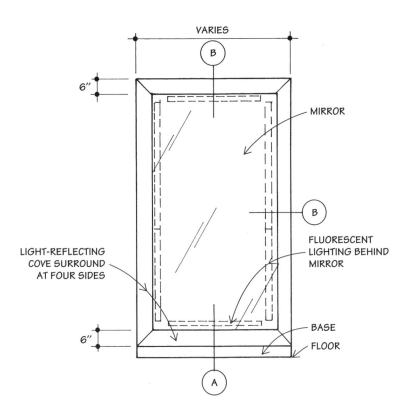

VARIES

B

6"

MIRROR

LIGHT-REFLECTING
COVE SURROUND
AT FOUR SIDES

FLUORESCENT
LIGHTING BEHIND
MIRROR

B

6"

BASE

FLOOR

A

**FITTING ROOM MIRROR ELEVATION**

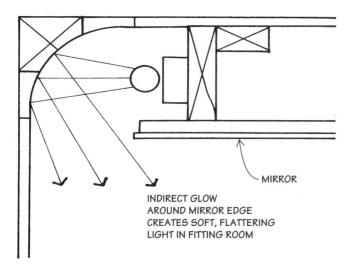

MIRROR

INDIRECT GLOW
AROUND MIRROR EDGE
CREATES SOFT, FLATTERING
LIGHT IN FITTING ROOM

**SIDE DETAIL, SECTION B**

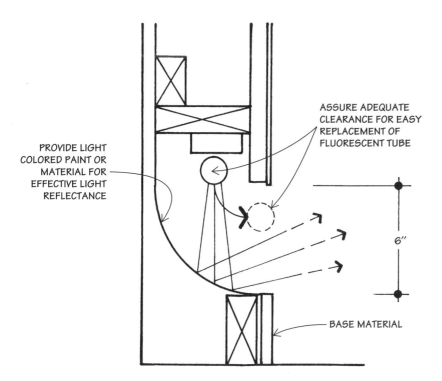

ASSURE ADEQUATE
CLEARANCE FOR EASY
REPLACEMENT OF
FLUORESCENT TUBE

PROVIDE LIGHT
COLORED PAINT OR
MATERIAL FOR
EFFECTIVE LIGHT
REFLECTANCE

6"

BASE MATERIAL

**BASE DETAIL, A**

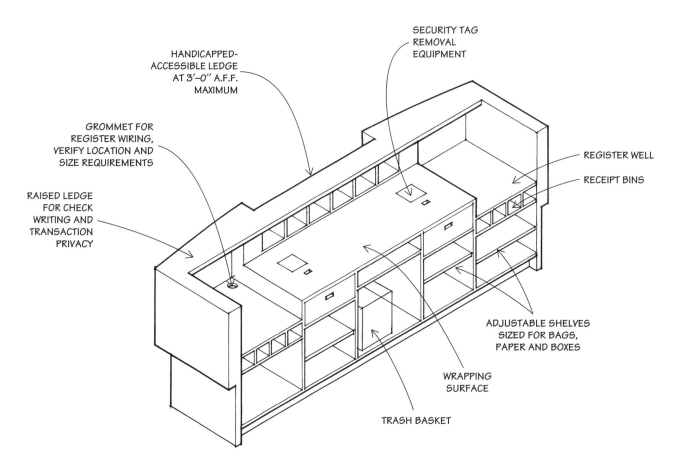

HANDICAPPED-
ACCESSIBLE LEDGE
AT 3'–0'' A.F.F.
MAXIMUM

SECURITY TAG
REMOVAL
EQUIPMENT

GROMMET FOR
REGISTER WIRING,
VERIFY LOCATION AND
SIZE REQUIREMENTS

REGISTER WELL

RECEIPT BINS

RAISED LEDGE
FOR CHECK
WRITING AND
TRANSACTION
PRIVACY

ADJUSTABLE SHELVES
SIZED FOR BAGS,
PAPER AND BOXES

WRAPPING
SURFACE

TRASH BASKET

**CASHWRAP**

# 2

# Men's Apparel Stores

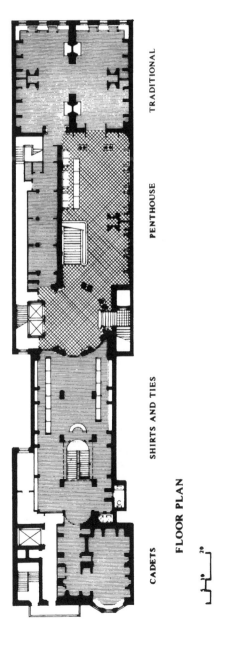

TRADITIONAL

PENTHOUSE

SHIRTS AND TIES

CADETS

FLOOR PLAN

10'  20'

**ONE FLOOR OF A FIVE-STORY MEN'S APPAREL STORE IN A RENOVATED BUILDING IN A DOWNTOWN URBAN LOCATION**

## Tips and Guidelines

1. Provide functional and interesting wall displays.

   - Consider both the wall design and the quantity of the merchandise to be contained within the storage units.
   - Men's clothing stores display more folded merchandise than is customarily found in women's apparel stores.

2. Fashion accessories are high-turnover, high-profit items.

   - Belts, socks, etc., should be positioned for impulse buying.

3. Men's stores may have a club fitting room area that includes space for alteration fitter.

4. Place lighting in wall units so that the light hits sleeves rather than the shoulders.

5. Attractive tie and shirt displays should be placed in feature-forward area to stimulate purchasing.

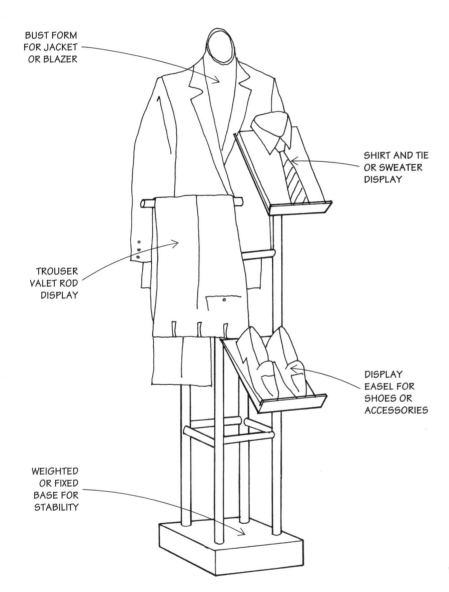

BUST FORM
FOR JACKET
OR BLAZER

SHIRT AND TIE
OR SWEATER
DISPLAY

TROUSER
VALET ROD
DISPLAY

DISPLAY
EASEL FOR
SHOES OR
ACCESSORIES

WEIGHTED
OR FIXED
BASE FOR
STABILITY

**WARDROBE DISPLAY**

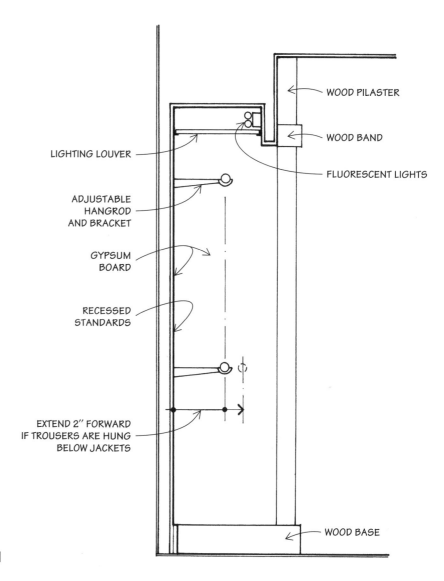

LIGHTING LOUVER

ADJUSTABLE
HANGROD
AND BRACKET

GYPSUM
BOARD

RECESSED
STANDARDS

EXTEND 2″ FORWARD
IF TROUSERS ARE HUNG
BELOW JACKETS

WOOD PILASTER

WOOD BAND

FLUORESCENT LIGHTS

WOOD BASE

**TYPICAL WALL CASE SECTION**

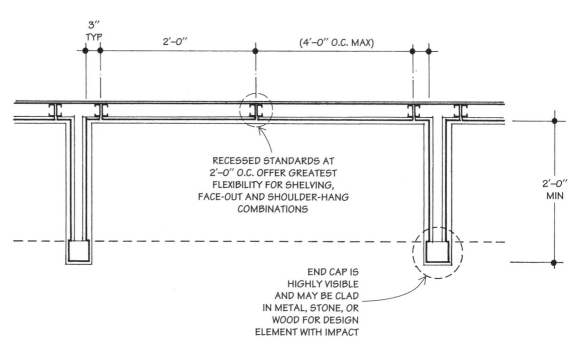

3″
TYP

2′-0″

(4′-0″ O.C. MAX)

RECESSED STANDARDS AT
2′-0″ O.C. OFFER GREATEST
FLEXIBILITY FOR SHELVING,
FACE-OUT AND SHOULDER-HANG
COMBINATIONS

2′-0″
MIN

END CAP IS
HIGHLY VISIBLE
AND MAY BE CLAD
IN METAL, STONE, OR
WOOD FOR DESIGN
ELEMENT WITH IMPACT

**PLAN VIEW, WALL CASE FOR HANGROD AND SHELVING**

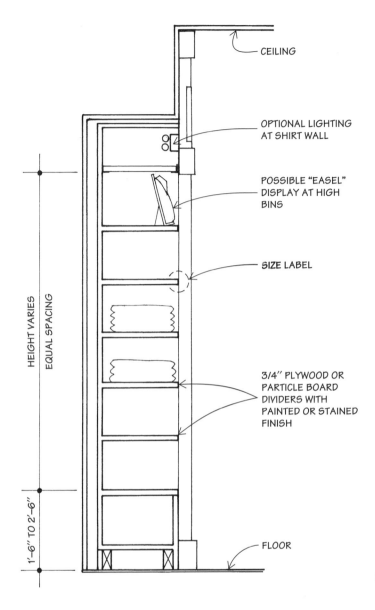

CEILING

OPTIONAL LIGHTING
AT SHIRT WALL

POSSIBLE "EASEL"
DISPLAY AT HIGH
BINS

SIZE LABEL

3/4" PLYWOOD OR
PARTICLE BOARD
DIVIDERS WITH
PAINTED OR STAINED
FINISH

FLOOR

HEIGHT VARIES

EQUAL SPACING

1'-6" TO 2'-6"

**SHIRT WALL DETAIL SECTION**

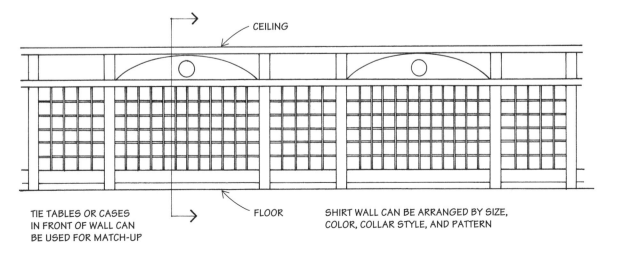

CEILING

FLOOR

TIE TABLES OR CASES
IN FRONT OF WALL CAN
BE USED FOR MATCH-UP

SHIRT WALL CAN BE ARRANGED BY SIZE,
COLOR, COLLAR STYLE, AND PATTERN

**SHIRT WALL ELEVATION**

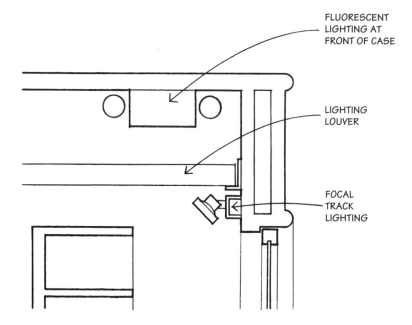

**DETAIL AT HEAD OF DISPLAY CASE**

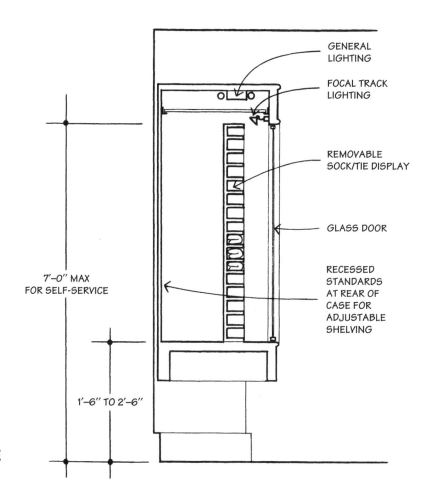

**WALL CASE WITH REMOVABLE
SOCK/TIE DISPLAY**

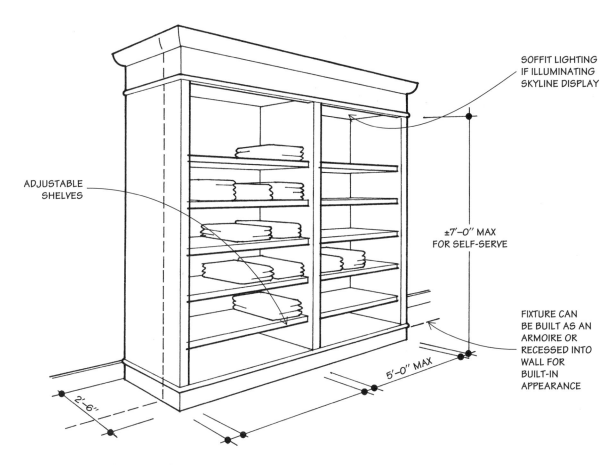

SOFFIT LIGHTING
IF ILLUMINATING
SKYLINE DISPLAY

ADJUSTABLE
SHELVES

±7'-0" MAX
FOR SELF-SERVE

FIXTURE CAN
BE BUILT AS AN
ARMOIRE OR
RECESSED INTO
WALL FOR
BUILT-IN
APPEARANCE

5'-0" MAX

2'-6"

**MERCHANDISE ARMOIRE**

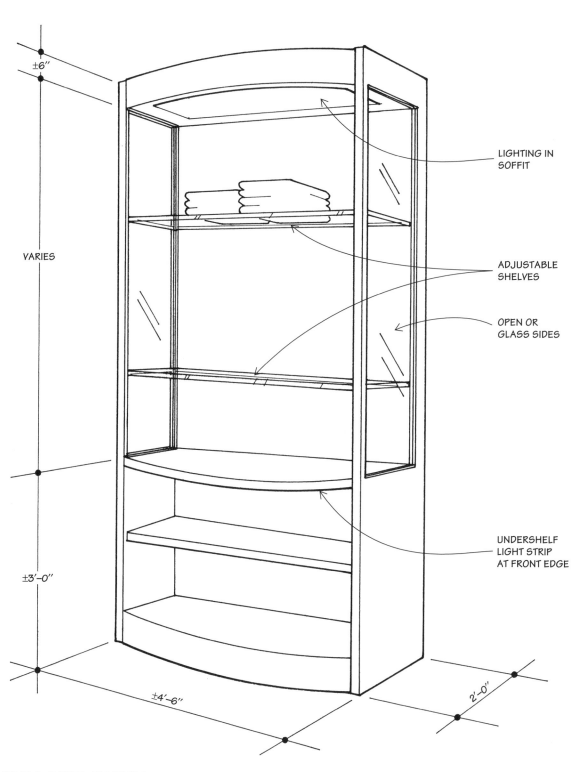

±6"

VARIES

±3'—0"

±4'—6"

2'—0"

LIGHTING IN
SOFFIT

ADJUSTABLE
SHELVES

OPEN OR
GLASS SIDES

UNDERSHELF
LIGHT STRIP
AT FRONT EDGE

**WALL DISPLAY UNIT**

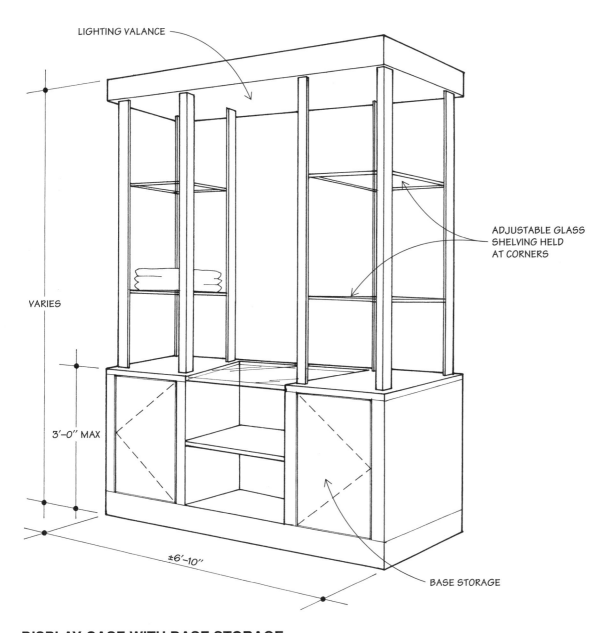

LIGHTING VALANCE

ADJUSTABLE GLASS
SHELVING HELD
AT CORNERS

VARIES

3'-0" MAX

±6'-10"

BASE STORAGE

## DISPLAY CASE WITH BASE STORAGE

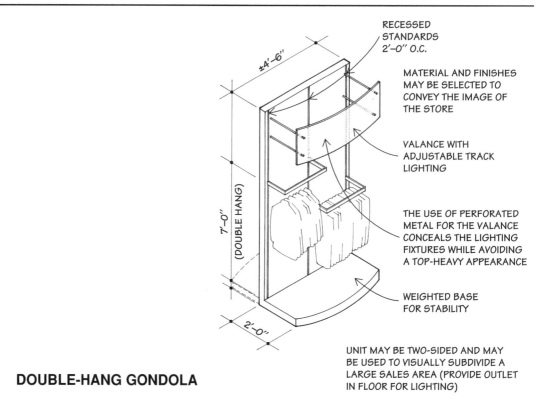

RECESSED
STANDARDS
2'-0" O.C.

MATERIAL AND FINISHES
MAY BE SELECTED TO
CONVEY THE IMAGE OF
THE STORE

VALANCE WITH
ADJUSTABLE TRACK
LIGHTING

THE USE OF PERFORATED
METAL FOR THE VALANCE
CONCEALS THE LIGHTING
FIXTURES WHILE AVOIDING
A TOP-HEAVY APPEARANCE

WEIGHTED BASE
FOR STABILITY

±4'-6"

7'-0"
(DOUBLE HANG)

2'-0"

UNIT MAY BE TWO-SIDED AND MAY
BE USED TO VISUALLY SUBDIVIDE A
LARGE SALES AREA (PROVIDE OUTLET
IN FLOOR FOR LIGHTING)

**DOUBLE-HANG GONDOLA**

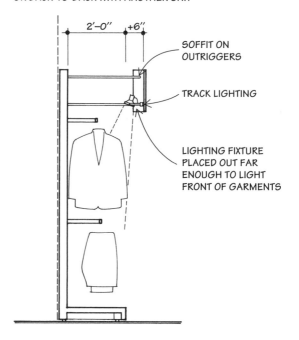

FIXTURE CAN BE LOCATED AGAINST WALL
OR BACK-TO-BACK WITH ANOTHER UNIT

2'-0"   +6"

SOFFIT ON
OUTRIGGERS

TRACK LIGHTING

LIGHTING FIXTURE
PLACED OUT FAR
ENOUGH TO LIGHT
FRONT OF GARMENTS

**SECTION, DOUBLE-HANG GONDOLA**

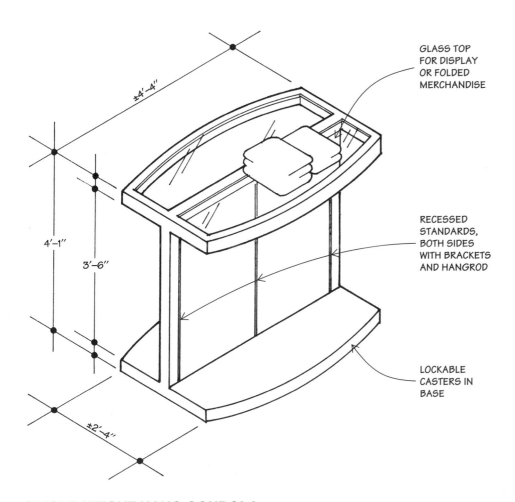

GLASS TOP
FOR DISPLAY
OR FOLDED
MERCHANDISE

±4'–4"

RECESSED
STANDARDS,
BOTH SIDES
WITH BRACKETS
AND HANGROD

4'–1"

3'–6"

LOCKABLE
CASTERS IN
BASE

±2'–4"

**SINGLE-HEIGHT HANG GONDOLA**

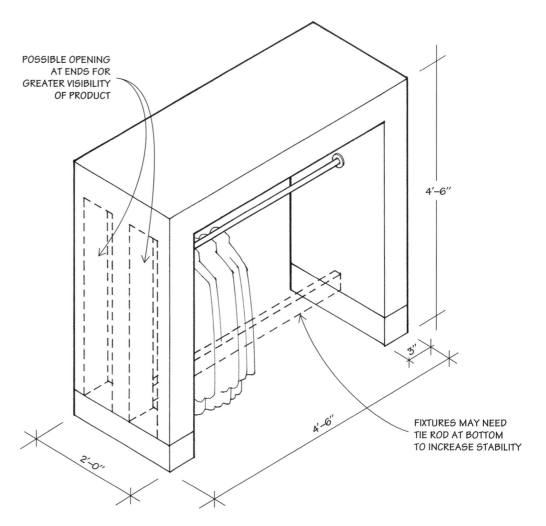

POSSIBLE OPENING
AT ENDS FOR
GREATER VISIBILITY
OF PRODUCT

4'-6"

3"

4'-6"

2'-0"

FIXTURES MAY NEED
TIE ROD AT BOTTOM
TO INCREASE STABILITY

**SUIT UNIT**

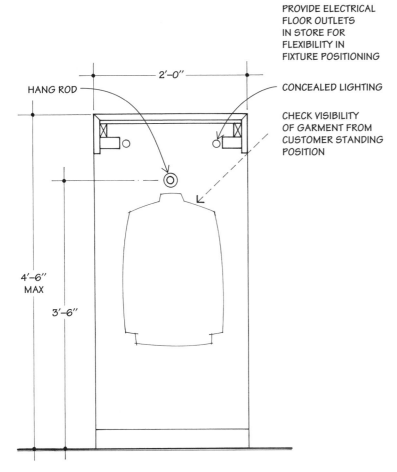

PROVIDE ELECTRICAL
FLOOR OUTLETS
IN STORE FOR
FLEXIBILITY IN
FIXTURE POSITIONING

HANG ROD

2'-0"

CONCEALED LIGHTING

CHECK VISIBILITY
OF GARMENT FROM
CUSTOMER STANDING
POSITION

4'-6"
MAX

3'-6"

**SECTION THROUGH SUIT UNIT**

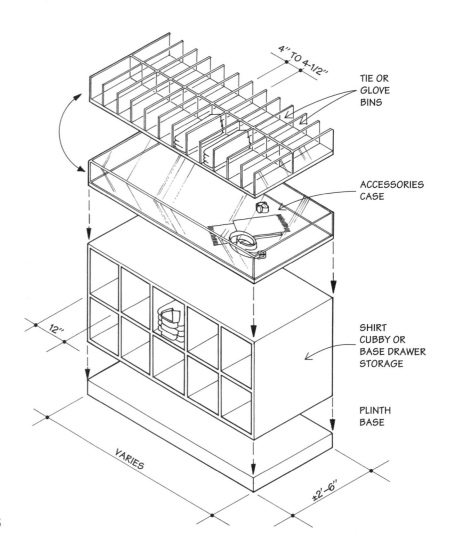

4" TO 4-1/2"

TIE OR GLOVE BINS

ACCESSORIES CASE

12"

SHIRT CUBBY OR BASE DRAWER STORAGE

PLINTH BASE

VARIES

±2'-6"

**ACCESSORY CASE WITH BINS**

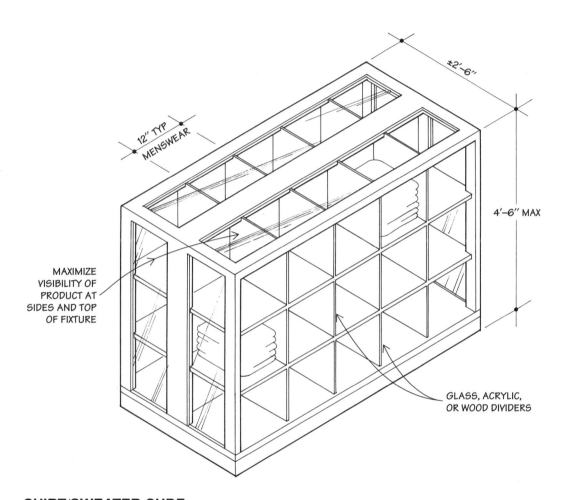

±2'-6"

12" TYP
MENSWEAR

4'-6" MAX

MAXIMIZE
VISIBILITY OF
PRODUCT AT
SIDES AND TOP
OF FIXTURE

GLASS, ACRYLIC,
OR WOOD DIVIDERS

## SHIRT/SWEATER CUBE

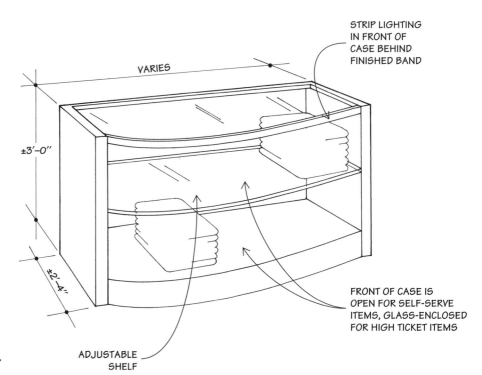

STRIP LIGHTING
IN FRONT OF
CASE BEHIND
FINISHED BAND

VARIES

±3'–0''

±2'–4''

FRONT OF CASE IS
OPEN FOR SELF-SERVE
ITEMS, GLASS-ENCLOSED
FOR HIGH TICKET ITEMS

ADJUSTABLE
SHELF

**LOW SHELVED UNIT**

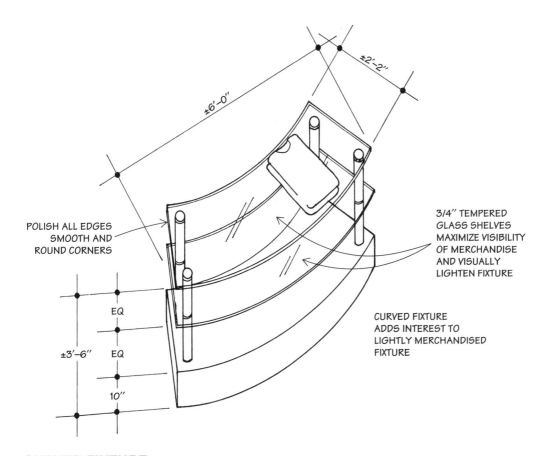

POLISH ALL EDGES
SMOOTH AND
ROUND CORNERS

±6'-0"

±2'-2"

EQ

±3'-6"    EQ

10"

3/4" TEMPERED
GLASS SHELVES
MAXIMIZE VISIBILITY
OF MERCHANDISE
AND VISUALLY
LIGHTEN FIXTURE

CURVED FIXTURE
ADDS INTEREST TO
LIGHTLY MERCHANDISED
FIXTURE

## CURVED FIXTURE

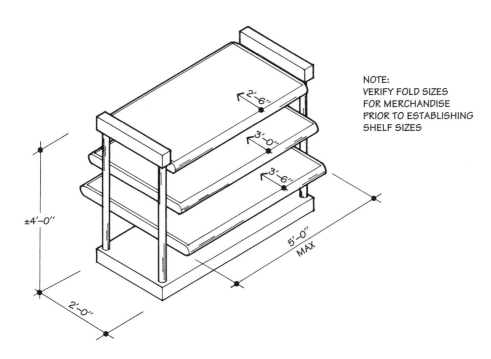

2'-6"

3'-0"

3'-6"

NOTE:
VERIFY FOLD SIZES
FOR MERCHANDISE
PRIOR TO ESTABLISHING
SHELF SIZES

±4'-0"

2'-0"

5'-0"
MAX

## DOUBLE-SIDED TIERED
## FIXTURE

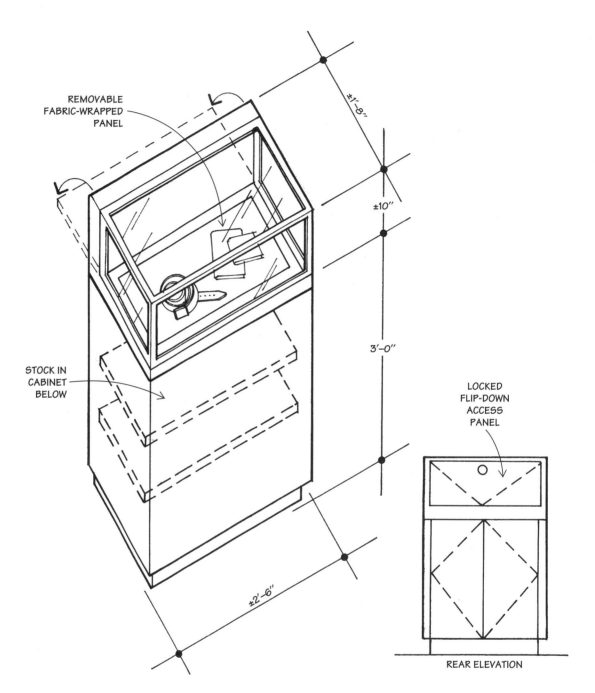

REMOVABLE
FABRIC-WRAPPED
PANEL

STOCK IN
CABINET
BELOW

±1'-8"

±10"

3'-0"

±2'-6"

LOCKED
FLIP-DOWN
ACCESS
PANEL

REAR ELEVATION

## ACCESSORY DISPLAY

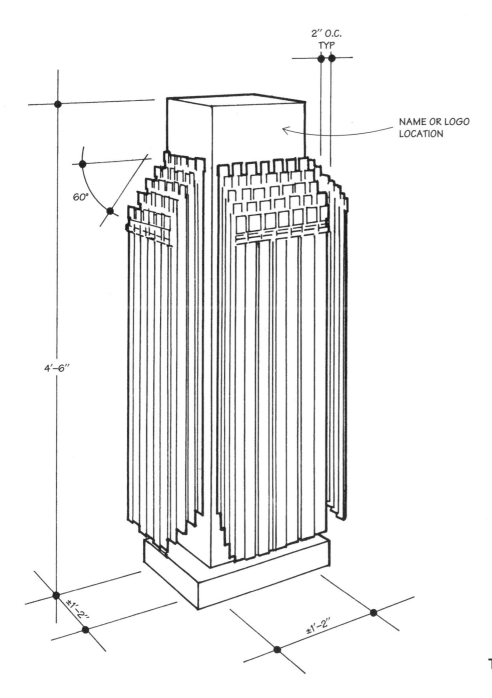

2" O.C.
TYP

NAME OR LOGO
LOCATION

60°

4'-6"

±1'-2"

±1'-2"

**TIERED BELT TOWER**

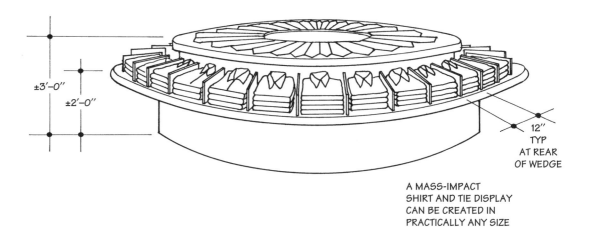

±3'-0"

±2'-0"

12"
TYP
AT REAR
OF WEDGE

A MASS-IMPACT
SHIRT AND TIE DISPLAY
CAN BE CREATED IN
PRACTICALLY ANY SIZE

**ROUND DISPLAY TABLE**

# 3

# Children's Apparel Stores

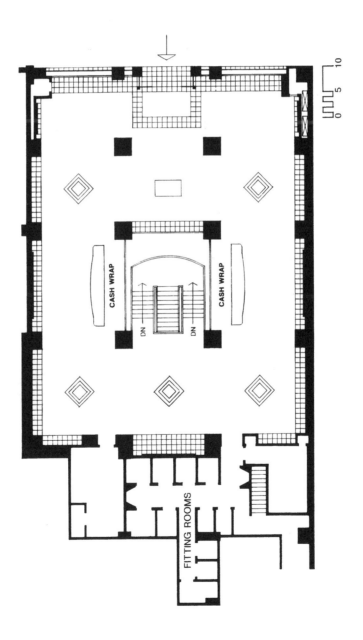

**TWO-LEVEL (GROUND AND FIRST FLOOR) CHILDREN'S APPAREL STORE IN A MULTI-STORY BUILDING IN AN URBAN LOCATION**

41

## Tips and Guidelines

1. Children's clothing and accessories items are typically selected by parents or grandparents.

   - Merchandise displays should be scaled for and accessible by adult shoppers.

2. Store interior should have a bright, up-beat, playful ambience.

3. Configure display units so that they do not pose a hazard to children.

   - Avoid sharp corners, protruding objects, exposed electric outlets, and breakable light fixtures.

4. Provide a safe area on the sales floor for game playing, reading, or watching television by children who are resting or waiting for accompanying adults.

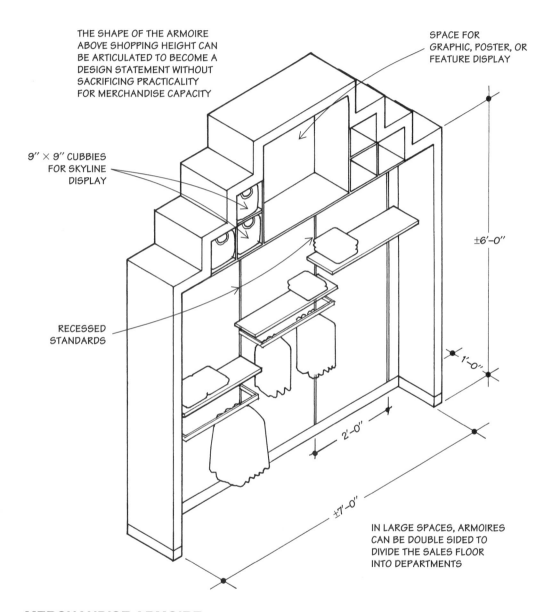

THE SHAPE OF THE ARMOIRE
ABOVE SHOPPING HEIGHT CAN
BE ARTICULATED TO BECOME A
DESIGN STATEMENT WITHOUT
SACRIFICING PRACTICALITY
FOR MERCHANDISE CAPACITY

SPACE FOR
GRAPHIC, POSTER, OR
FEATURE DISPLAY

9″ × 9″ CUBBIES
FOR SKYLINE
DISPLAY

±6′-0″

RECESSED
STANDARDS

1′-0″

2′-0″

±7′-0″

IN LARGE SPACES, ARMOIRES
CAN BE DOUBLE SIDED TO
DIVIDE THE SALES FLOOR
INTO DEPARTMENTS

# MERCHANDISE ARMOIRE

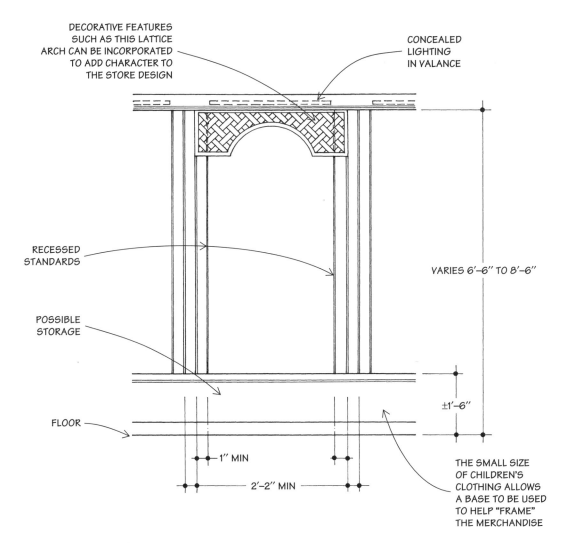

DECORATIVE FEATURES
SUCH AS THIS LATTICE
ARCH CAN BE INCORPORATED
TO ADD CHARACTER TO
THE STORE DESIGN

CONCEALED
LIGHTING
IN VALANCE

RECESSED
STANDARDS

VARIES 6'-6" TO 8'-6"

POSSIBLE
STORAGE

FLOOR

±1'-6"

1" MIN

2'-2" MIN

THE SMALL SIZE
OF CHILDREN'S
CLOTHING ALLOWS
A BASE TO BE USED
TO HELP "FRAME"
THE MERCHANDISE

**WALL ELEVATION**

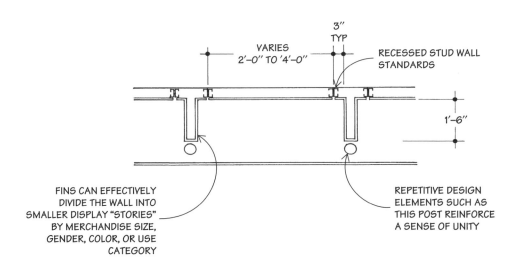

VARIES
2'-0" TO '4'-0"

3"
TYP

RECESSED STUD WALL
STANDARDS

1'-6"

FINS CAN EFFECTIVELY
DIVIDE THE WALL INTO
SMALLER DISPLAY "STORIES"
BY MERCHANDISE SIZE,
GENDER, COLOR, OR USE
CATEGORY

REPETITIVE DESIGN
ELEMENTS SUCH AS
THIS POST REINFORCE
A SENSE OF UNITY

**WALL RECESS PLAN**

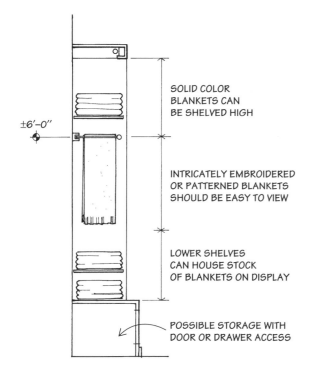

±6'-0"

SOLID COLOR
BLANKETS CAN
BE SHELVED HIGH

INTRICATELY EMBROIDERED
OR PATTERNED BLANKETS
SHOULD BE EASY TO VIEW

LOWER SHELVES
CAN HOUSE STOCK
OF BLANKETS ON DISPLAY

POSSIBLE STORAGE WITH
DOOR OR DRAWER ACCESS

**SECTION OF BLANKET/SHAWL DISPLAY**

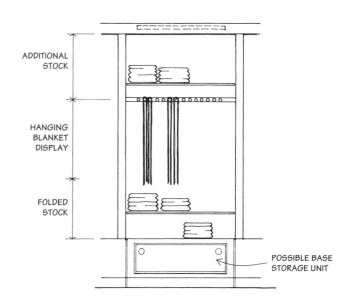

ADDITIONAL
STOCK

HANGING
BLANKET
DISPLAY

FOLDED
STOCK

POSSIBLE BASE
STORAGE UNIT

**ELEVATION OF BLANKET/SHAWL DISPLAY**

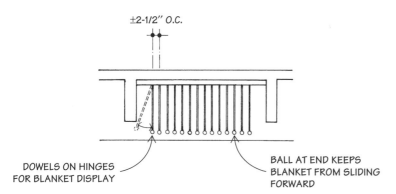

±2-1/2" O.C.

DOWELS ON HINGES
FOR BLANKET DISPLAY

BALL AT END KEEPS
BLANKET FROM SLIDING
FORWARD

**PLAN OF BLANKET/SHAWL DISPLAY**

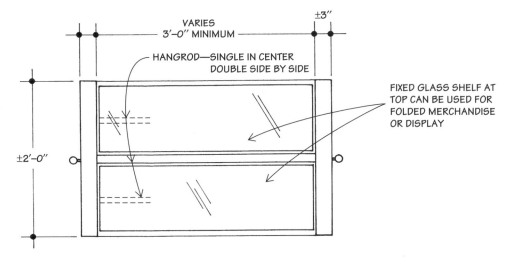

VARIES
3'-0" MINIMUM

±3"

HANGROD—SINGLE IN CENTER
DOUBLE SIDE BY SIDE

FIXED GLASS SHELF AT
TOP CAN BE USED FOR
FOLDED MERCHANDISE
OR DISPLAY

±2'-0"

**PLAN OF GONDOLA**

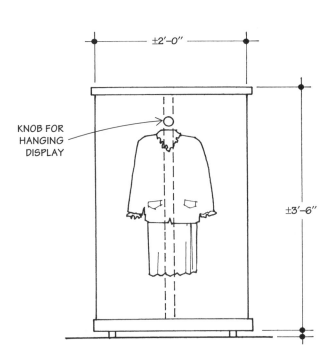

±2'-0"

KNOB FOR
HANGING
DISPLAY

±3'-6"

**SIDE ELEVATION OF GONDOLA**

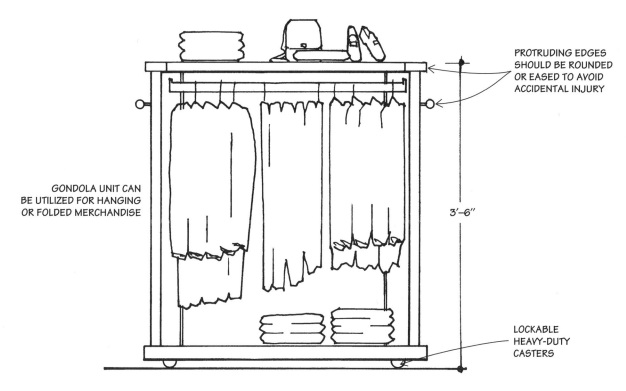

PROTRUDING EDGES
SHOULD BE ROUNDED
OR EASED TO AVOID
ACCIDENTAL INJURY

GONDOLA UNIT CAN
BE UTILIZED FOR HANGING
OR FOLDED MERCHANDISE

3'–6"

LOCKABLE
HEAVY-DUTY
CASTERS

**FRONT ELEVATION OF GONDOLA**

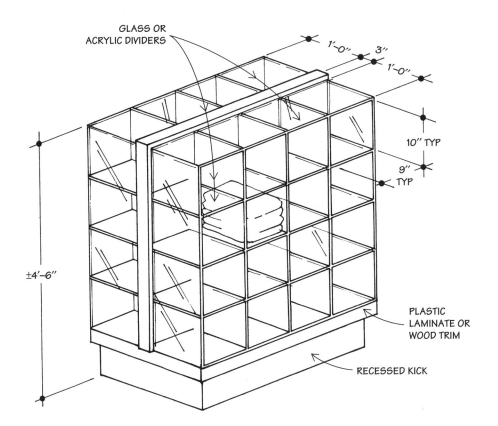

GLASS OR
ACRYLIC DIVIDERS

1'-0"    3"
1'-0"

10" TYP

9"
TYP

±4'-6"

PLASTIC
LAMINATE OR
WOOD TRIM

RECESSED KICK

**FOLDED MERCHANDISE CUBICLE FIXTURE**

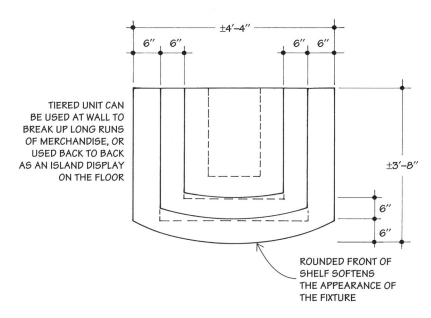

±4'-4"

6"  6"          6"  6"

±3'-8"

6"

6"

TIERED UNIT CAN
BE USED AT WALL TO
BREAK UP LONG RUNS
OF MERCHANDISE, OR
USED BACK TO BACK
AS AN ISLAND DISPLAY
ON THE FLOOR

ROUNDED FRONT OF
SHELF SOFTENS
THE APPEARANCE OF
THE FIXTURE

**PLAN OF TIERED UNIT**

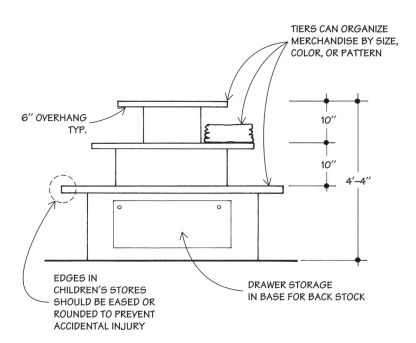

TIERS CAN ORGANIZE
MERCHANDISE BY SIZE,
COLOR, OR PATTERN

6" OVERHANG
TYP.

10"

10"

4'-4"

EDGES IN
CHILDREN'S STORES
SHOULD BE EASED OR
ROUNDED TO PREVENT
ACCIDENTAL INJURY

DRAWER STORAGE
IN BASE FOR BACK STOCK

**ELEVATION OF TIERED UNIT**

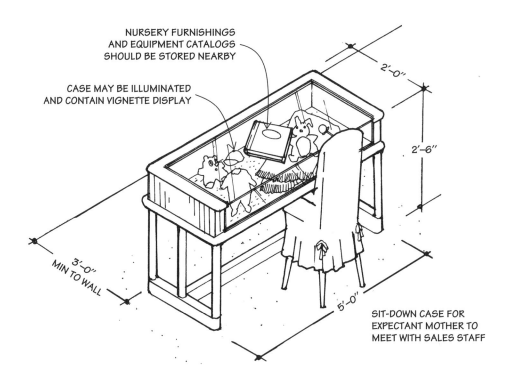

NURSERY FURNISHINGS
AND EQUIPMENT CATALOGS
SHOULD BE STORED NEARBY

CASE MAY BE ILLUMINATED
AND CONTAIN VIGNETTE DISPLAY

2'-0"

2'-6"

3'-0"
MIN TO WALL

5'-0"

SIT-DOWN CASE FOR
EXPECTANT MOTHER TO
MEET WITH SALES STAFF

**SIT-DOWN CASE**

# 4

# Shoe Stores

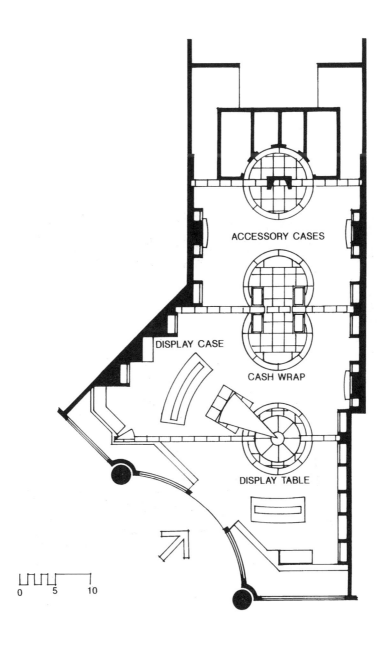

ACCESSORY CASES

DISPLAY CASE

CASH WRAP

DISPLAY TABLE

**SINGLE-LEVEL SHOE STORE CARRYING MID-PRICE MERCHANDISE, LOCATED IN A REGIONAL MALL**

0    5    10

## Tips and Guidelines

1. Shoe stores for men, women, and children fall into two categories: traditional service operations with salespeople and hidden stock, or self-service with all stock placed on the selling floor near style samples.

2. Shoe store profit is linked to:

   - Size of stock room and amount of inventory carried.

   - Number of seats in relation to dollar amount of sales generated.

   - Turnover of merchandise.

3. Appealing merchandise displays invite customer product examination.

   - Specify movable display units, such as tables and pedestals, and built-ins, such as niches and wall-mounted shelving.

4. For retail shoe operations, lighting should be planned to spotlight displays in windows and vignettes.

5. Seating areas for customers to try on shoes should be convenient and comfortable.

   - Banquettes, benches, loveseats, and chairs can be utilized.

6. Provide full-length mirrors rather than small, floor-level mirrors that show only the customer's feet.

   - Larger mirrors show the merchandise in proportion to the customer's body and in relation to individual style and functional needs.

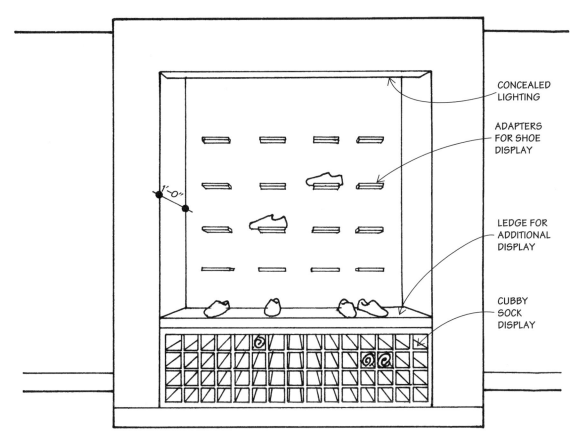

**WALL SHOE AND SOCK DISPLAY**

CONCEALED LIGHTING

ADAPTERS FOR SHOE DISPLAY

LEDGE FOR ADDITIONAL DISPLAY

CUBBY SOCK DISPLAY

1'-0"

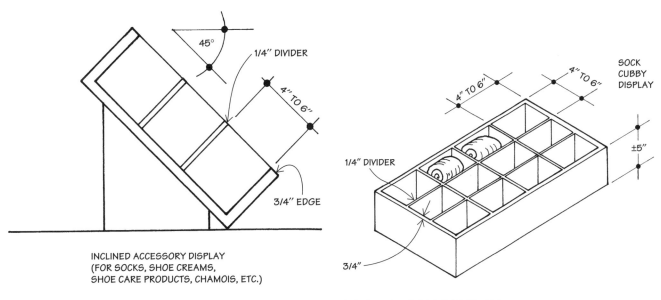

45°

1/4" DIVIDER

4" TO 6"

3/4" EDGE

INCLINED ACCESSORY DISPLAY
(FOR SOCKS, SHOE CREAMS,
SHOE CARE PRODUCTS, CHAMOIS, ETC.)

**SECTION**

SOCK CUBBY DISPLAY

4" TO 6"

4" TO 6"

±5"

1/4" DIVIDER

3/4"

**SOCK CUBBY DISPLAY**

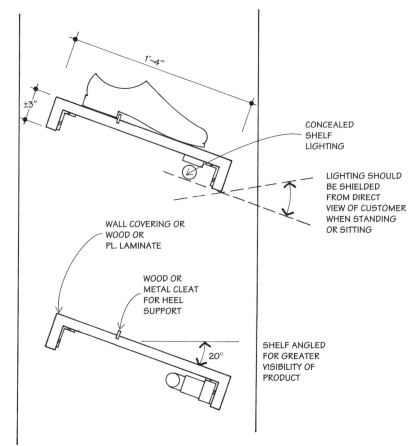

1'-4"

±3"

CONCEALED
SHELF
LIGHTING

LIGHTING SHOULD
BE SHIELDED
FROM DIRECT
VIEW OF CUSTOMER
WHEN STANDING
OR SITTING

WALL COVERING OR
WOOD OR
PL. LAMINATE

WOOD OR
METAL CLEAT
FOR HEEL
SUPPORT

20°

SHELF ANGLED
FOR GREATER
VISIBILITY OF
PRODUCT

**WALL SECTION OF SHOE DISPLAY**

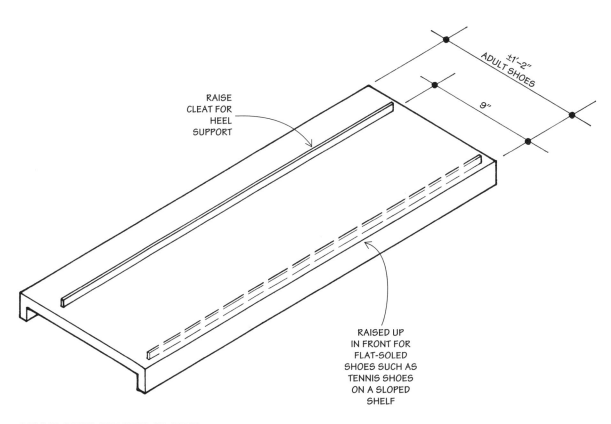

±1'-2"
ADULT SHOES

9"

RAISE
CLEAT FOR
HEEL
SUPPORT

RAISED UP
IN FRONT FOR
FLAT-SOLED
SHOES SUCH AS
TENNIS SHOES
ON A SLOPED
SHELF

**SHOE SHELF WITH CLEAT**

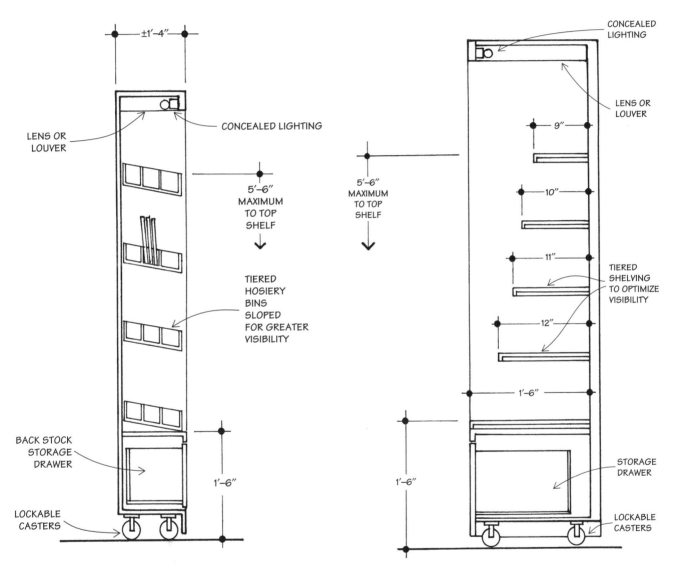

**PANTY-HOSE UNIT**

**MOVABLE SHOE ÉTAGÈRE**

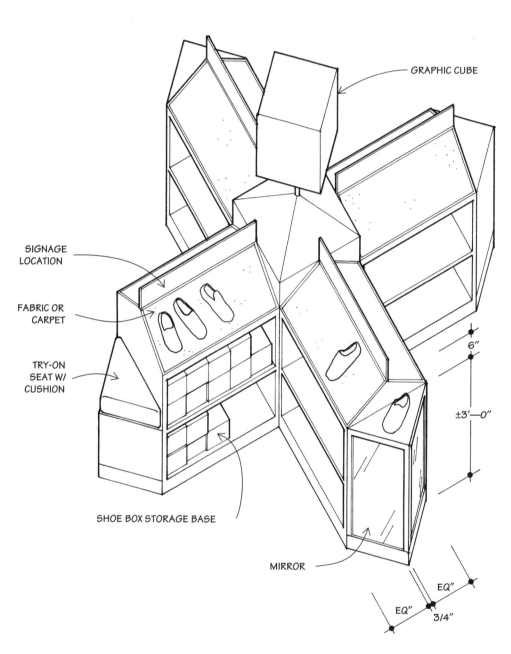

GRAPHIC CUBE

SIGNAGE
LOCATION

FABRIC OR
CARPET

TRY-ON
SEAT W/
CUSHION

SHOE BOX STORAGE BASE

MIRROR

6"

±3'—0"

EQ"

EQ"

3/4"

**SELF-SERVICE SHOE DISPLAY WITH
STORAGE SEAT AND MIRRORS**

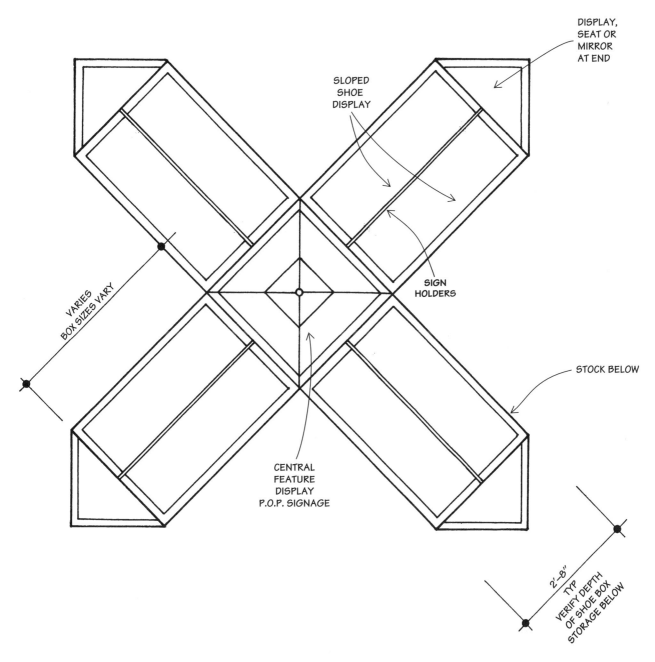

DISPLAY,
SEAT OR
MIRROR
AT END

SLOPED
SHOE
DISPLAY

SIGN
HOLDERS

VARIES
BOX SIZES VARY

STOCK BELOW

CENTRAL
FEATURE
DISPLAY
P.O.P. SIGNAGE

2'-8"
TYP
VERIFY DEPTH
OF SHOE BOX
STORAGE BELOW

**PLAN**

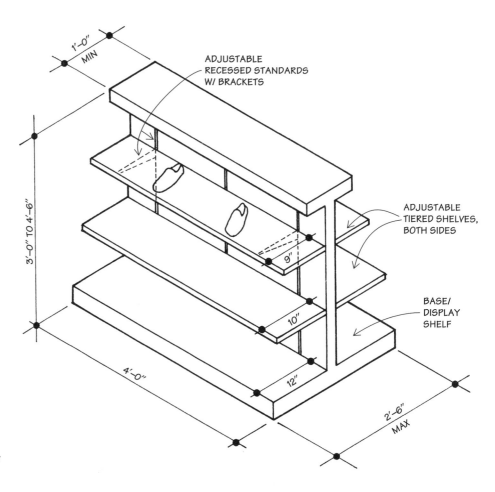

ADJUSTABLE
RECESSED STANDARDS
W/ BRACKETS

ADJUSTABLE
TIERED SHELVES,
BOTH SIDES

BASE/
DISPLAY
SHELF

1'-0"
MIN

3'-0" TO 4'-6"

9"

10"

12"

4'-0"

2'-6"
MAX

**SHOE DISPLAY**

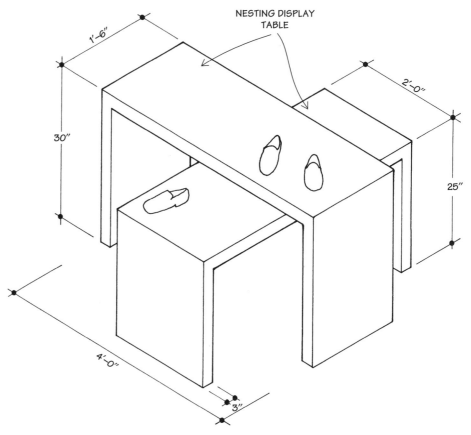

NESTING DISPLAY
TABLE

1'-6"

2'-0"

30"

25"

4'-0"

3"

**NESTING TABLES**

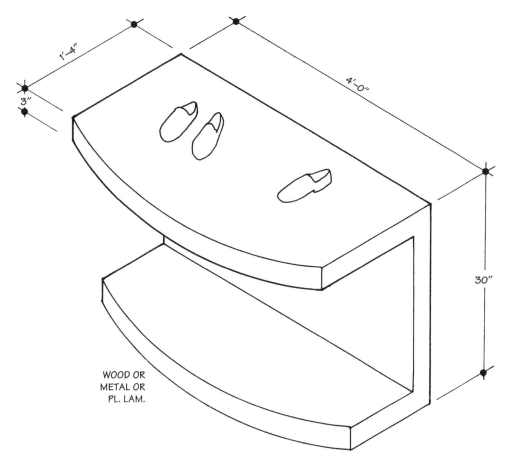

**SHOE AND ACCESSORY DISPLAY TABLE**

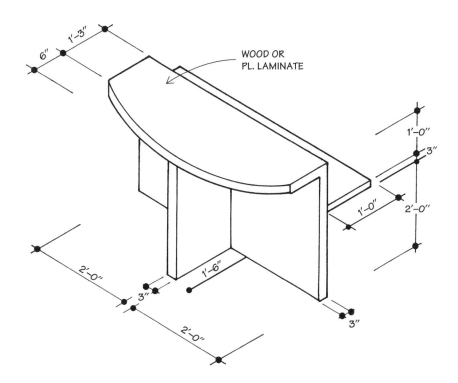

**SHOE DISPLAY TABLE**

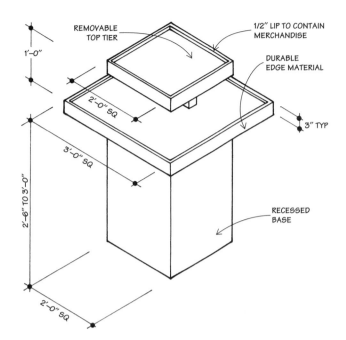

REMOVABLE
TOP TIER

1/2" LIP TO CONTAIN
MERCHANDISE

DURABLE
EDGE MATERIAL

1'-0"

2'-0" SQ

3" TYP

3'-0" SQ

2'-6" TO 3'-0"

RECESSED
BASE

2'-0" SQ

**FLOOR SHOE DISPLAY, TIER TOP**

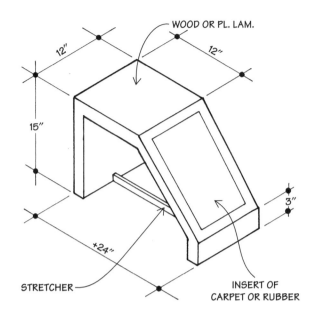

WOOD OR PL. LAM.

12"

12"

15"

3"

+24"

STRETCHER

INSERT OF
CARPET OR RUBBER

**SHOE TRY-ON STOOL**

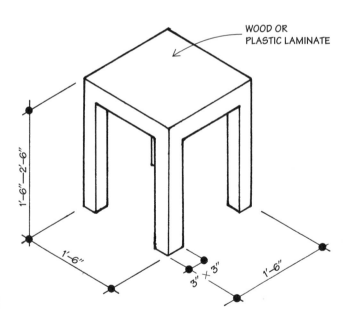

WOOD OR
PLASTIC LAMINATE

1'-6"—2'-6"

1'-6"

3" × 3"

1'-6"

**DISPLAY PEDESTAL OR TABLE**

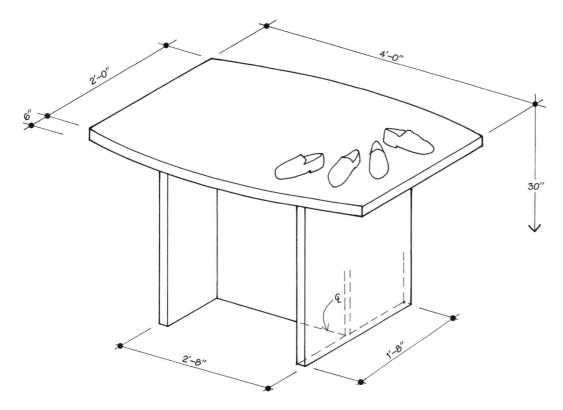

2'-0"

4'-0"

6"

30"

2'-8"

1'-8"

℄

**SHOE TABLE**

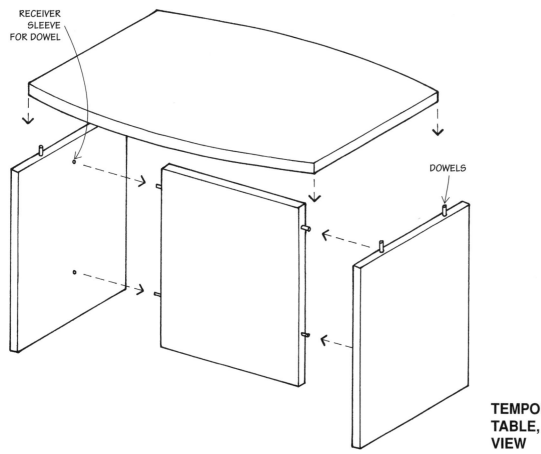

RECEIVER
SLEEVE
FOR DOWEL

DOWELS

**TEMPORARY SALE
TABLE, EXPLODED
VIEW**

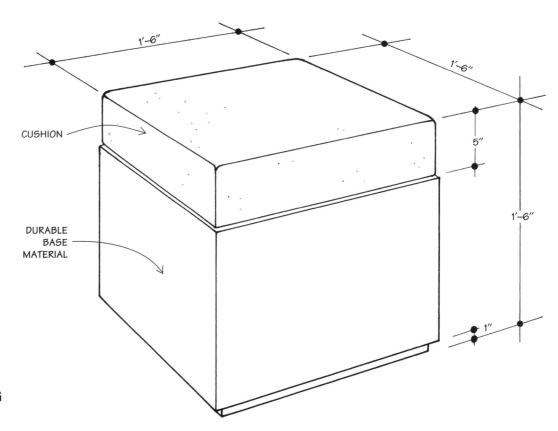

1'-6"

1'-6"

5"

1'-6"

1"

CUSHION

DURABLE
BASE
MATERIAL

**SHOE SEATING
CUBE**

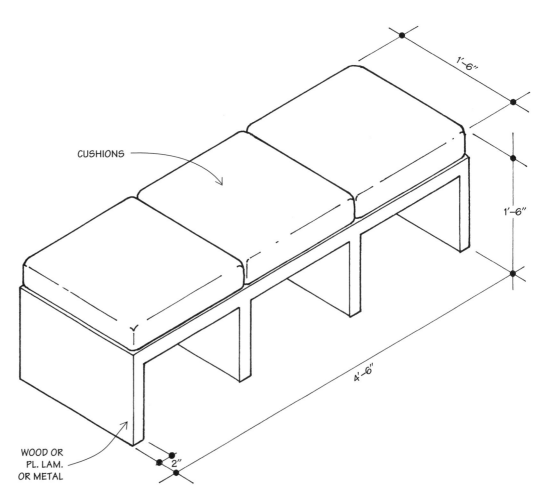

1'-6"

1'-6"

4'-6"

2"

CUSHIONS

WOOD OR
PL. LAM.
OR METAL

**SHOE BENCH**

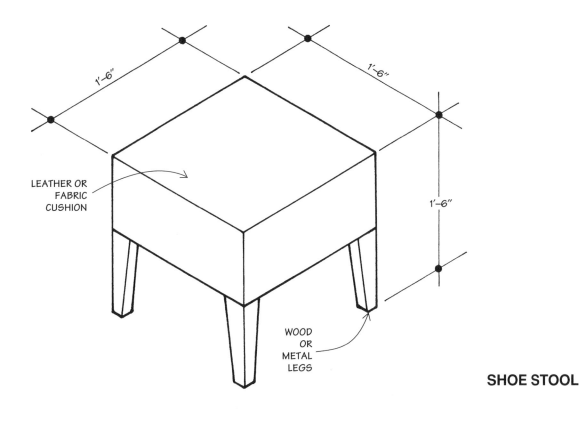

LEATHER OR
FABRIC
CUSHION

1'-6"

1'-6"

1'-6"

WOOD
OR
METAL
LEGS

**SHOE STOOL**

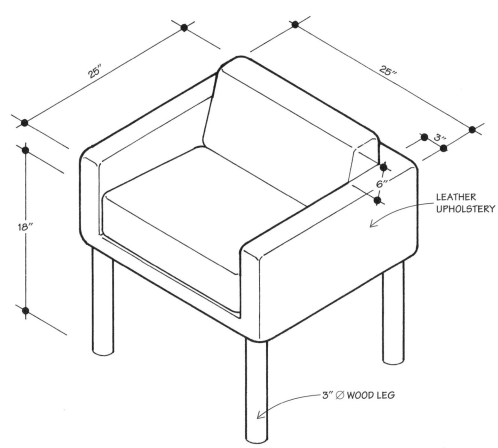

25"

25"

3"

6"

18"

LEATHER
UPHOLSTERY

3" Ø WOOD LEG

**SHOE SEAT**

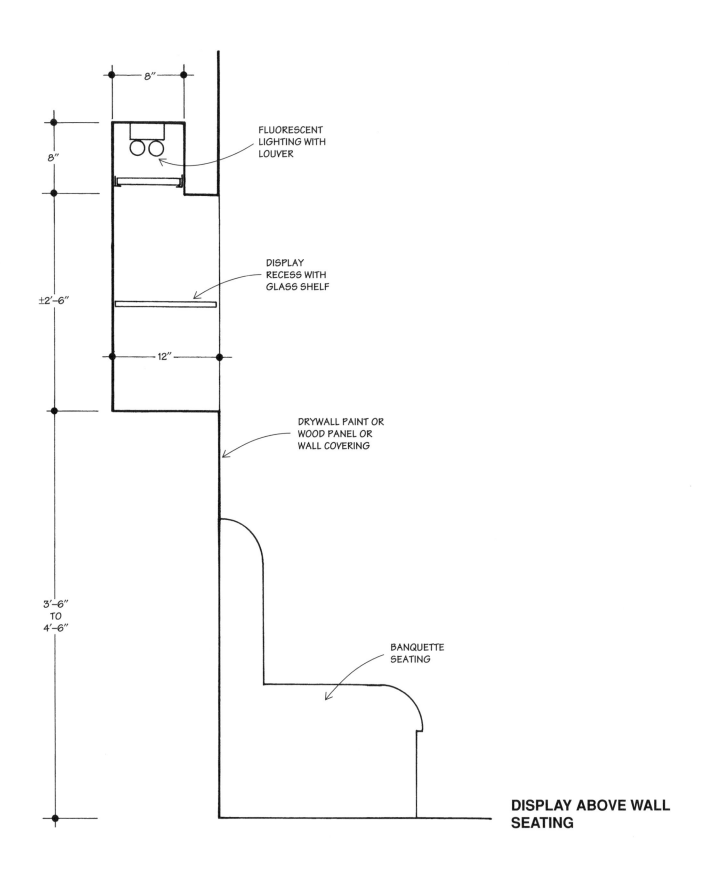

8″

8″

FLUORESCENT
LIGHTING WITH
LOUVER

±2′–6″

DISPLAY
RECESS WITH
GLASS SHELF

12″

DRYWALL PAINT OR
WOOD PANEL OR
WALL COVERING

3′–6″
TO
4′–6″

BANQUETTE
SEATING

**DISPLAY ABOVE WALL
SEATING**

# Discount Marts

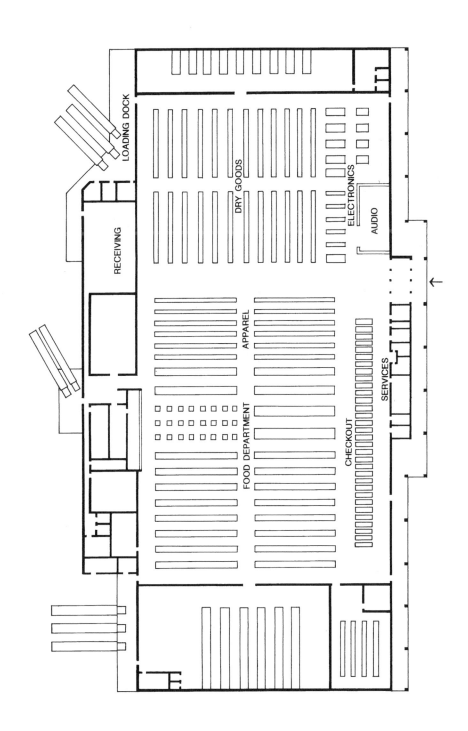

**FREE-STANDING
DISCOUNT STORE**

## Tips and Guidelines

1. Graphic design program should be planned to inform shoppers how the store is divided into selling zones.

   - Since most discount marts are self-service operations, merchandise signs should indicate price and terms of payment, product's benefits, new features, and other selling points.

2. Promoted as one-stop shopping destination and carry large inventories.

   - Appeal on basis of price and value.

3. Provide office and conference space for customer-relations activities.

4. HVAC engineering designs should employ energy-efficient systems.

   - Payback of co-generation, energy control systems, and other energy conservation and monitoring techniques should be determined.

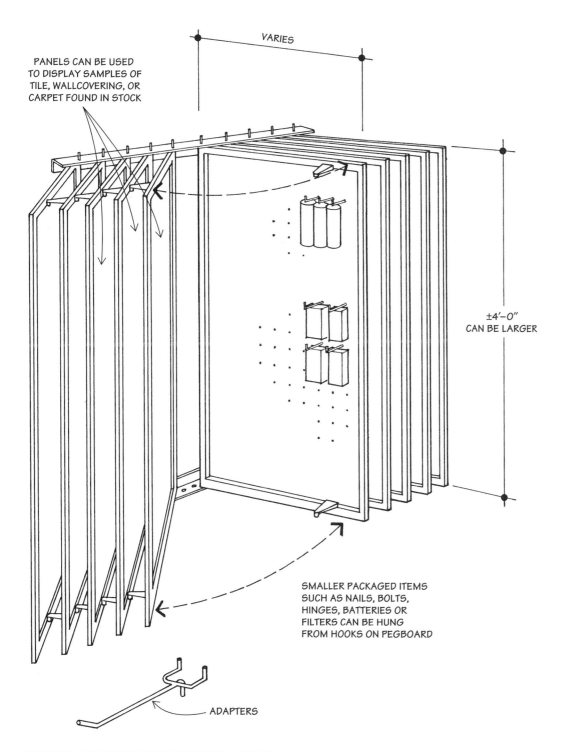

PANELS CAN BE USED
TO DISPLAY SAMPLES OF
TILE, WALLCOVERING, OR
CARPET FOUND IN STOCK

VARIES

±4'-0"
CAN BE LARGER

SMALLER PACKAGED ITEMS
SUCH AS NAILS, BOLTS,
HINGES, BATTERIES OR
FILTERS CAN BE HUNG
FROM HOOKS ON PEGBOARD

ADAPTERS

**SWIVEL PANELS FOR MERCHANDISE**

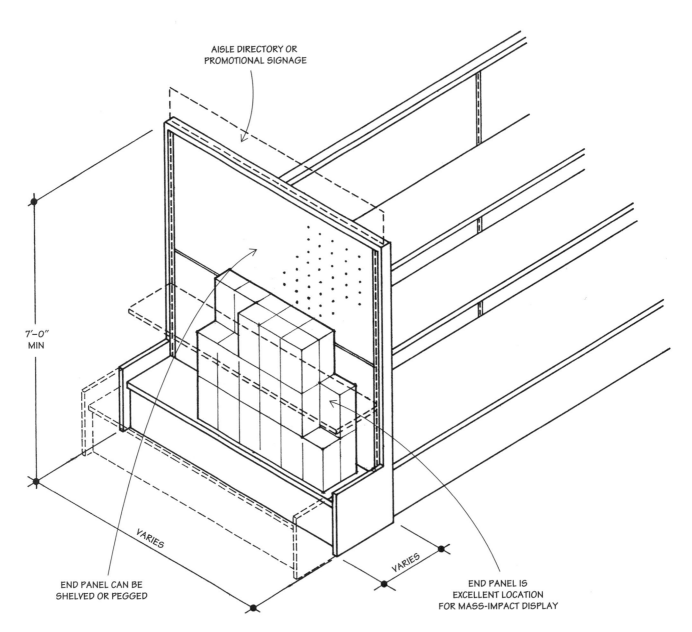

AISLE DIRECTORY OR
PROMOTIONAL SIGNAGE

7'-0"
MIN

VARIES

VARIES

END PANEL CAN BE
SHELVED OR PEGGED

END PANEL IS
EXCELLENT LOCATION
FOR MASS-IMPACT DISPLAY

**SHELVING UNIT END-CAP**

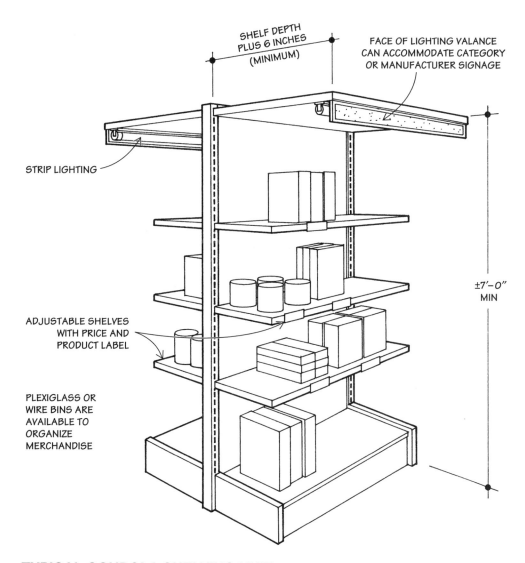

SHELF DEPTH
PLUS 6 INCHES
(MINIMUM)

FACE OF LIGHTING VALANCE
CAN ACCOMMODATE CATEGORY
OR MANUFACTURER SIGNAGE

STRIP LIGHTING

±7'-0"
MIN

ADJUSTABLE SHELVES
WITH PRICE AND
PRODUCT LABEL

PLEXIGLASS OR
WIRE BINS ARE
AVAILABLE TO
ORGANIZE
MERCHANDISE

## TYPICAL GONDOLA SHELVING UNIT

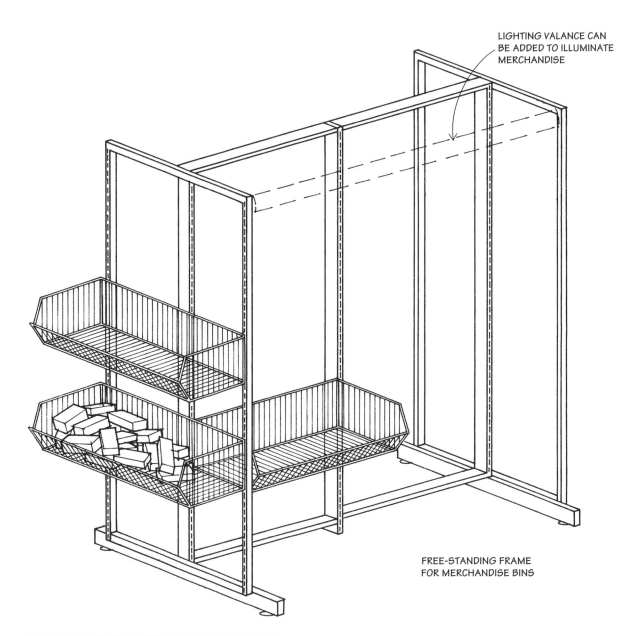

LIGHTING VALANCE CAN
BE ADDED TO ILLUMINATE
MERCHANDISE

FREE-STANDING FRAME
FOR MERCHANDISE BINS

**FREE-STANDING WIRE BASKET UNIT**

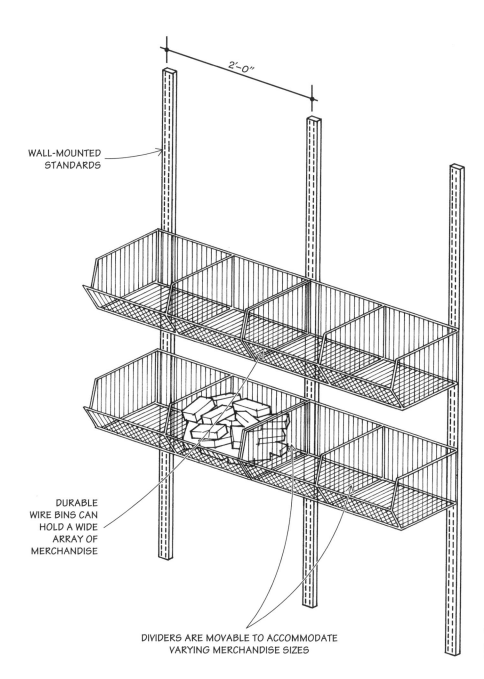

2'-0"

WALL-MOUNTED
STANDARDS

DURABLE
WIRE BINS CAN
HOLD A WIDE
ARRAY OF
MERCHANDISE

DIVIDERS ARE MOVABLE TO ACCOMMODATE
VARYING MERCHANDISE SIZES

**WALL-MOUNTED WIRE
BASKET UNITS**

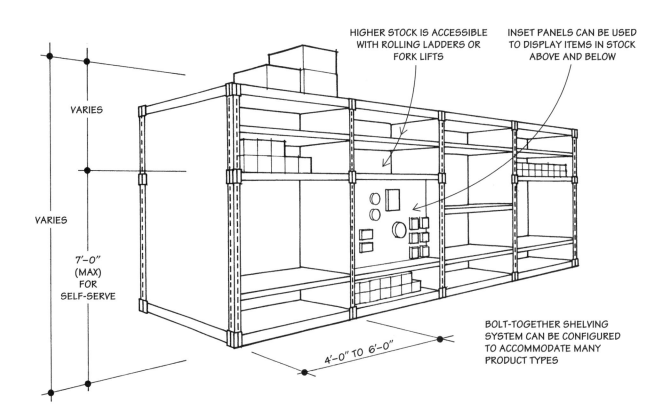

VARIES

VARIES

7'-0"
(MAX)
FOR
SELF-SERVE

HIGHER STOCK IS ACCESSIBLE
WITH ROLLING LADDERS OR
FORK LIFTS

INSET PANELS CAN BE USED
TO DISPLAY ITEMS IN STOCK
ABOVE AND BELOW

BOLT-TOGETHER SHELVING
SYSTEM CAN BE CONFIGURED
TO ACCOMMODATE MANY
PRODUCT TYPES

4'-0" TO 6'-0"

**LARGE SHELVING SYSTEM**

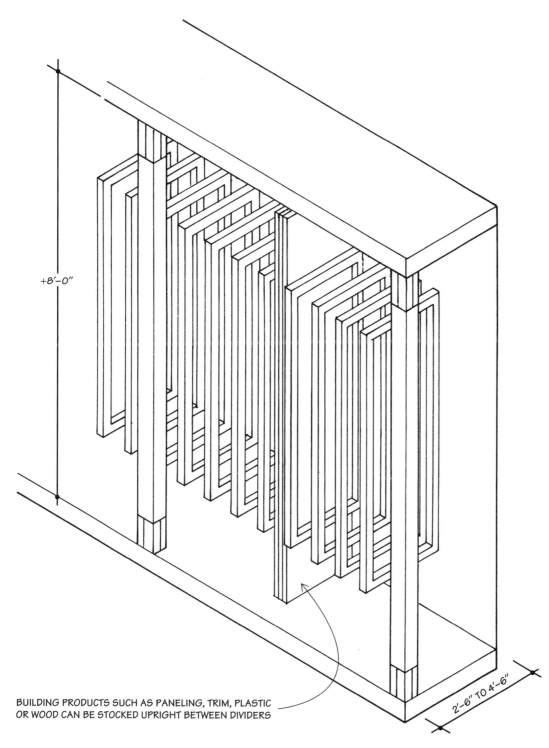

+8'–0"

2'–6" TO 4'–6"

BUILDING PRODUCTS SUCH AS PANELING, TRIM, PLASTIC
OR WOOD CAN BE STOCKED UPRIGHT BETWEEN DIVIDERS

## VERTICAL PANELS MERCHANDISE UNIT

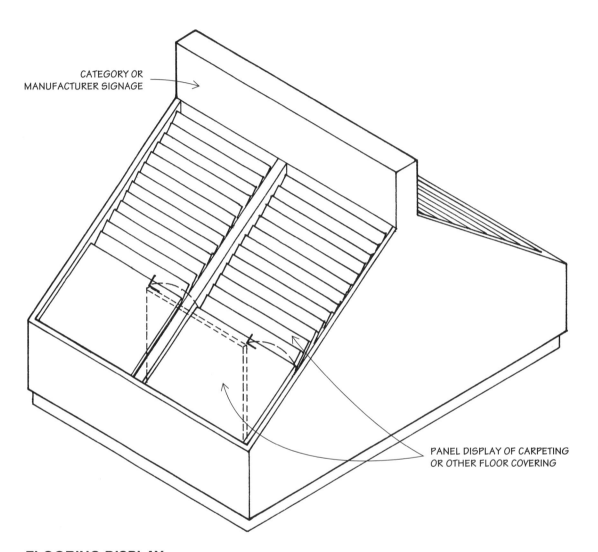

CATEGORY OR
MANUFACTURER SIGNAGE

PANEL DISPLAY OF CARPETING
OR OTHER FLOOR COVERING

**FLOORING DISPLAY**

# 6

# Drug Stores

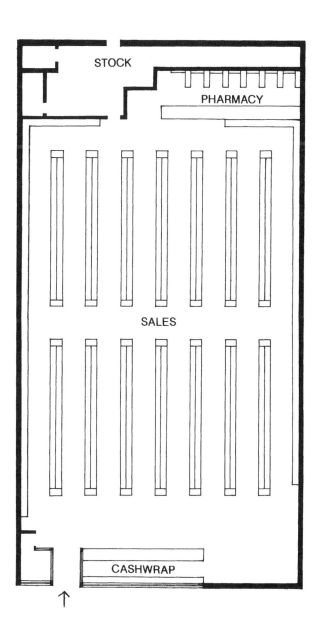

STOCK

PHARMACY

SALES

CASHWRAP

**BASIC LAYOUT FOR A
SINGLE-LEVEL CHAIN
DRUG STORE**

## Tips and Guidelines

1. Merchandise assortment of "super" drug stores can be nearly as large as the selections carried by the average supermarket.
2. Signs are very important.
   - Directional.
   - Merchandise identification and price.
3. For self-service selection, merchandise is displayed on shelves, racks, and gondolas.
4. Drug-dispensing area requires separate provision for security and for cashwrap surface.
   - Locked area to store certain prescription products.
5. To accommodate shopping carts, aisle width should be six to seven feet.

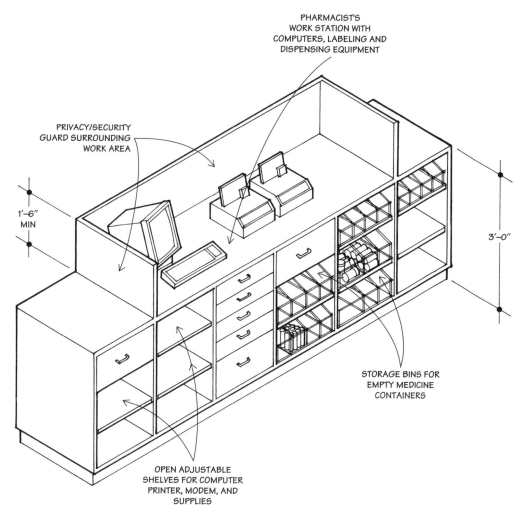

PHARMACIST'S
WORK STATION WITH
COMPUTERS, LABELING AND
DISPENSING EQUIPMENT

PRIVACY/SECURITY
GUARD SURROUNDING
WORK AREA

1'-6"
MIN

3'-0"

STORAGE BINS FOR
EMPTY MEDICINE
CONTAINERS

OPEN ADJUSTABLE
SHELVES FOR COMPUTER
PRINTER, MODEM, AND
SUPPLIES

**PHARMACY
COUNTER,
EMPLOYEE SIDE**

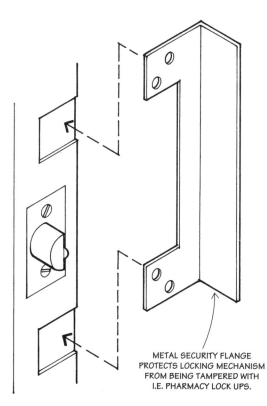

METAL SECURITY FLANGE
PROTECTS LOCKING MECHANISM
FROM BEING TAMPERED WITH
I.E. PHARMACY LOCK UPS.

**TAMPER-PROOF LOCKS**

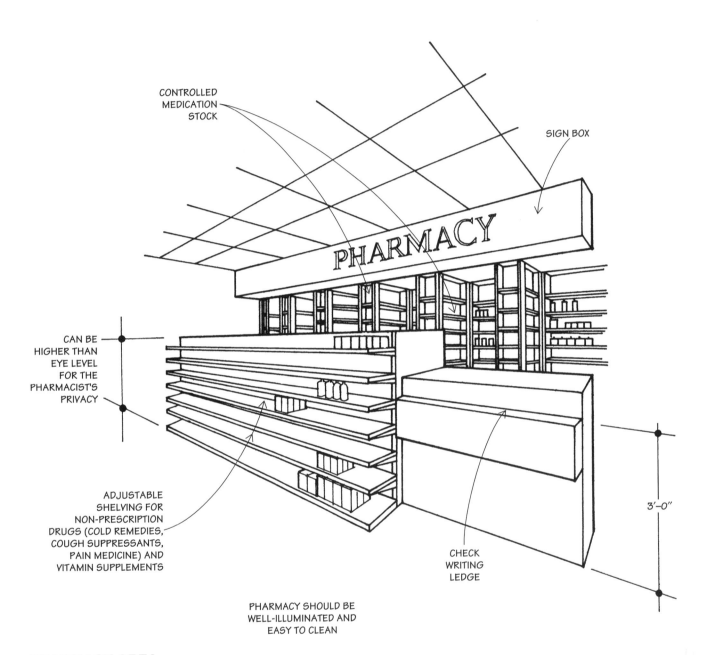

CONTROLLED MEDICATION STOCK

SIGN BOX

PHARMACY

CAN BE HIGHER THAN EYE LEVEL FOR THE PHARMACIST'S PRIVACY

3'-0"

ADJUSTABLE SHELVING FOR NON-PRESCRIPTION DRUGS (COLD REMEDIES, COUGH SUPPRESSANTS, PAIN MEDICINE) AND VITAMIN SUPPLEMENTS

CHECK WRITING LEDGE

PHARMACY SHOULD BE WELL-ILLUMINATED AND EASY TO CLEAN

## PHARMACY AREA

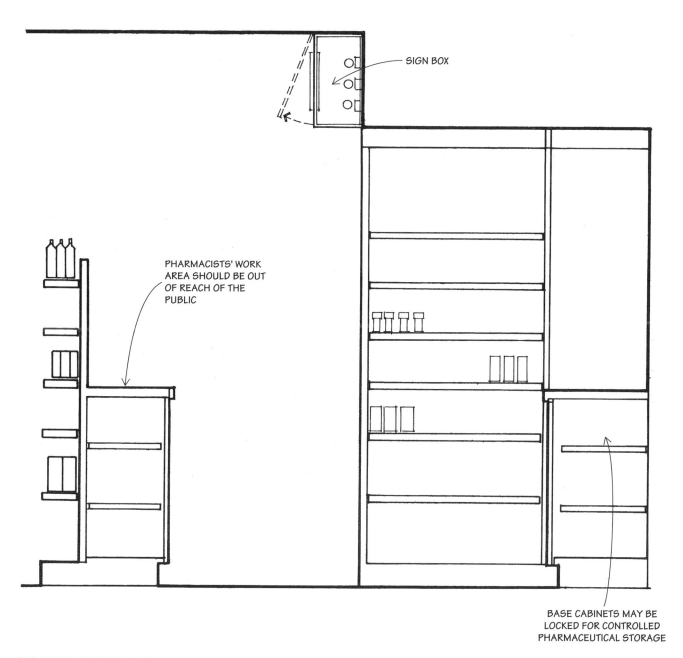

SIGN BOX

PHARMACISTS' WORK
AREA SHOULD BE OUT
OF REACH OF THE
PUBLIC

BASE CABINETS MAY BE
LOCKED FOR CONTROLLED
PHARMACEUTICAL STORAGE

# PHARMACISTS' WORK AREA

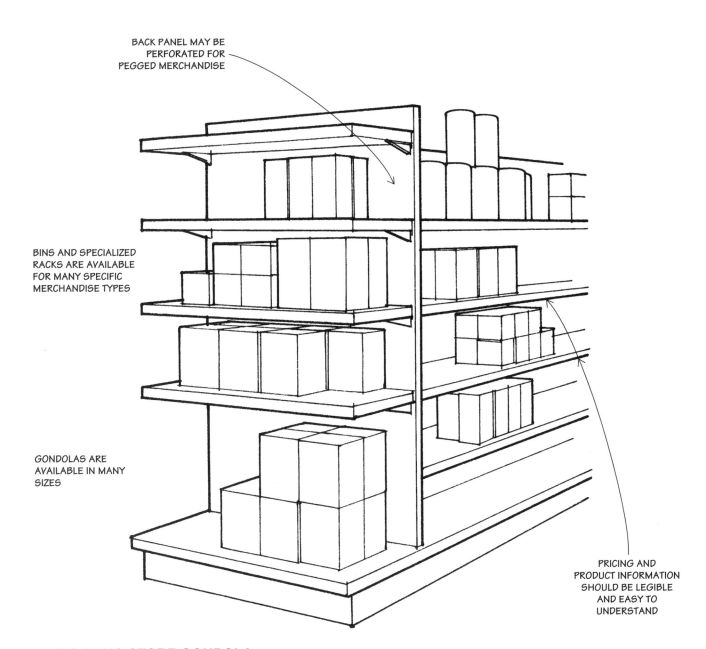

BACK PANEL MAY BE
PERFORATED FOR
PEGGED MERCHANDISE

BINS AND SPECIALIZED
RACKS ARE AVAILABLE
FOR MANY SPECIFIC
MERCHANDISE TYPES

GONDOLAS ARE
AVAILABLE IN MANY
SIZES

PRICING AND
PRODUCT INFORMATION
SHOULD BE LEGIBLE
AND EASY TO
UNDERSTAND

**BASIC DRUG STORE GONDOLA**

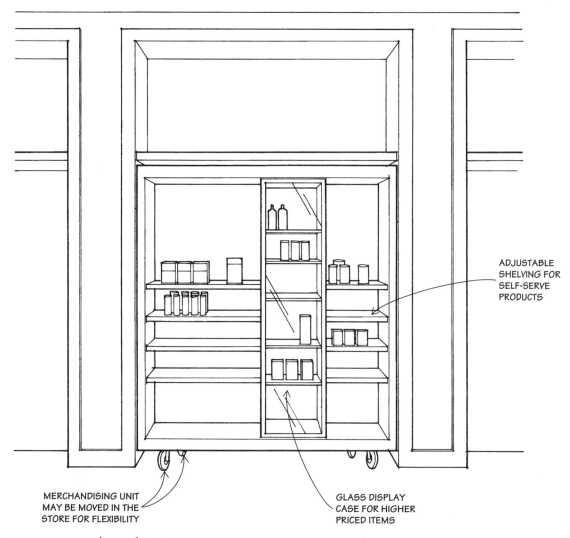

ADJUSTABLE
SHELVING FOR
SELF-SERVE
PRODUCTS

MERCHANDISING UNIT
MAY BE MOVED IN THE
STORE FOR FLEXIBILITY

GLASS DISPLAY
CASE FOR HIGHER
PRICED ITEMS

## PORTABLE ÉTAGÈRE

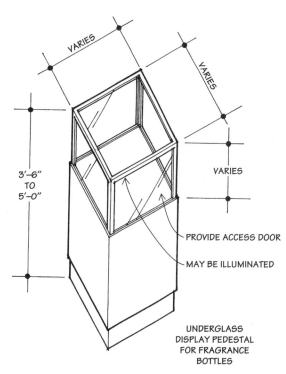

VARIES

VARIES

VARIES

3'–6"
TO
5'–0"

PROVIDE ACCESS DOOR

MAY BE ILLUMINATED

UNDERGLASS
DISPLAY PEDESTAL
FOR FRAGRANCE
BOTTLES

## FRAGRANCE DISPLAY CASE

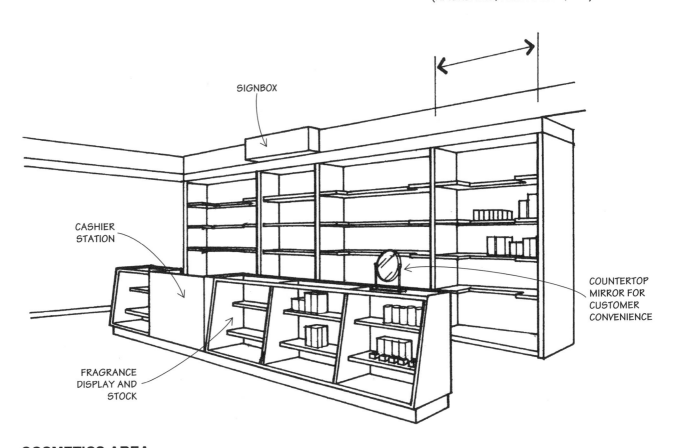

AREA CAN FEATURE
A MANUFACTURER'S LINE
OF PRODUCTS OR A
CATEGORY OF MERCHANDISE
(AFTERSHAVE, FACE POWDER, ETC.)

SIGNBOX

CASHIER
STATION

COUNTERTOP
MIRROR FOR
CUSTOMER
CONVENIENCE

FRAGRANCE
DISPLAY AND
STOCK

**COSMETICS AREA**

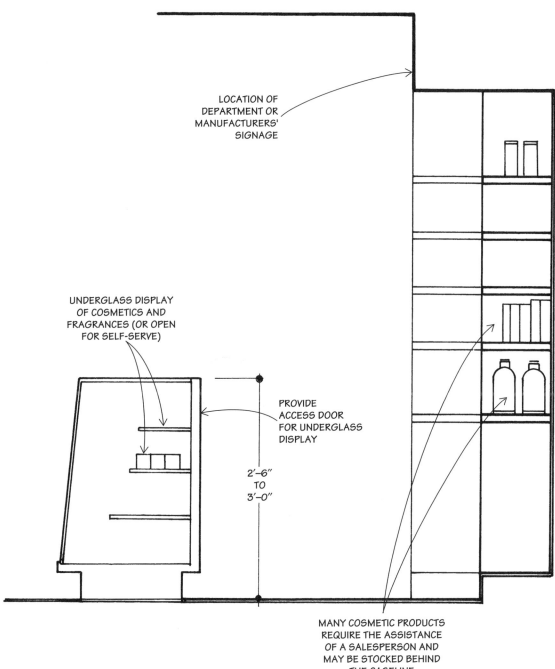

LOCATION OF
DEPARTMENT OR
MANUFACTURERS'
SIGNAGE

UNDERGLASS DISPLAY
OF COSMETICS AND
FRAGRANCES (OR OPEN
FOR SELF-SERVE)

PROVIDE
ACCESS DOOR
FOR UNDERGLASS
DISPLAY

2'–6"
TO
3'–0"

MANY COSMETIC PRODUCTS
REQUIRE THE ASSISTANCE
OF A SALESPERSON AND
MAY BE STOCKED BEHIND
THE CASELINE

## SECTION AT COSMETICS COUNTER

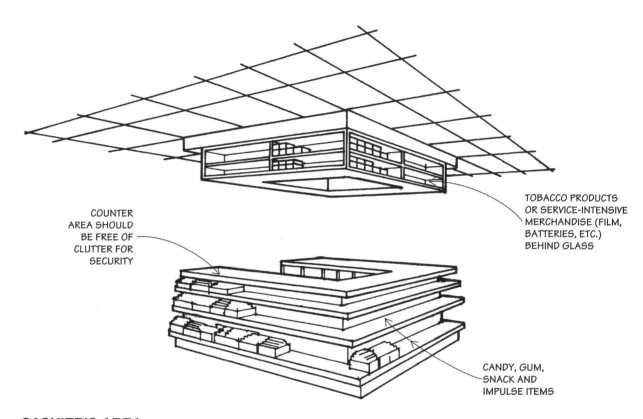

COUNTER
AREA SHOULD
BE FREE OF
CLUTTER FOR
SECURITY

TOBACCO PRODUCTS
OR SERVICE-INTENSIVE
MERCHANDISE (FILM,
BATTERIES, ETC.)
BEHIND GLASS

CANDY, GUM,
SNACK AND
IMPULSE ITEMS

## CASHIER'S AREA

# Food Markets

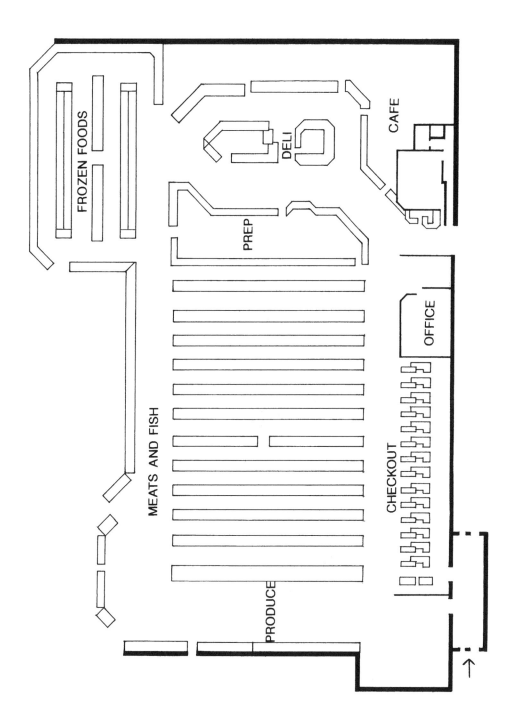

**FOOD MARKET WITH RESTAURANT**

FROZEN FOODS

CAFE

DELI

PREP

MEATS AND FISH

OFFICE

CHECKOUT

PRODUCE

## Tips and Guidelines

1. New trend in food marketing is positioning for customers' lifestyle orientation.
2. Expanded merchandise lines displayed on the selling floor have boosted some stores to 100,000 square feet and over.
   - Some become like self-contained mini-malls.
   - Shoppers can take advantage of in-store bakery, salad bars, prepared take-out foods, charcuteries, gourmet departments.
   - Kiosks for coffee, frozen yogurt, etc.
3. Services are new major category at larger supermarkets.
   - Banking, shoe repair, dry cleaning, one-hour photo service.
   - Video rental section.
4. Separate bulk purchase areas.
   - Displays highlight carton and case purchasing.
5. Be creative with signs.
   - Utilize neon and animated techniques to capture customer attention.

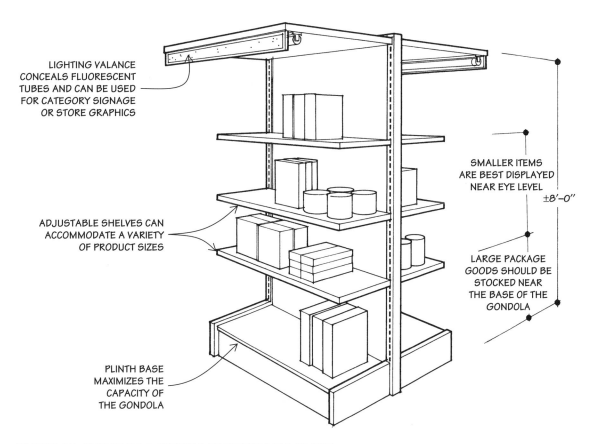

LIGHTING VALANCE
CONCEALS FLUORESCENT
TUBES AND CAN BE USED
FOR CATEGORY SIGNAGE
OR STORE GRAPHICS

SMALLER ITEMS
ARE BEST DISPLAYED
NEAR EYE LEVEL

±8'-0"

ADJUSTABLE SHELVES CAN
ACCOMMODATE A VARIETY
OF PRODUCT SIZES

LARGE PACKAGE
GOODS SHOULD BE
STOCKED NEAR
THE BASE OF THE
GONDOLA

PLINTH BASE
MAXIMIZES THE
CAPACITY OF
THE GONDOLA

**TYPICAL GONDOLA WITH LIGHTED VALANCE**

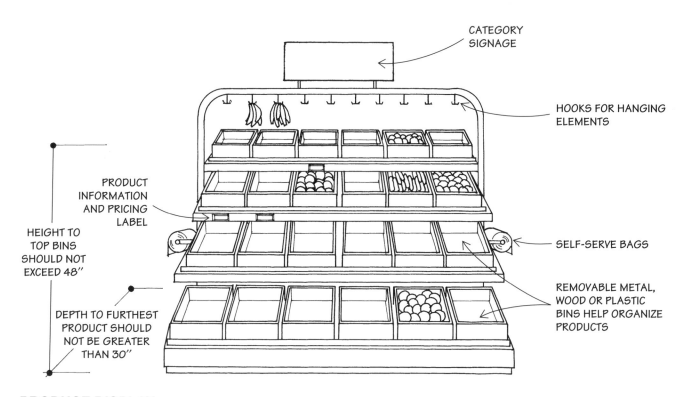

CATEGORY
SIGNAGE

HOOKS FOR HANGING
ELEMENTS

PRODUCT
INFORMATION
AND PRICING
LABEL

HEIGHT TO
TOP BINS
SHOULD NOT
EXCEED 48"

SELF-SERVE BAGS

REMOVABLE METAL,
WOOD OR PLASTIC
BINS HELP ORGANIZE
PRODUCTS

DEPTH TO FURTHEST
PRODUCT SHOULD
NOT BE GREATER
THAN 30"

## PRODUCE DISPLAY

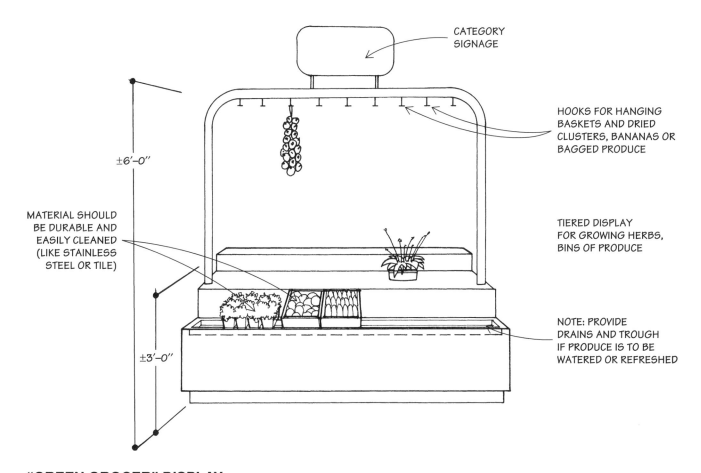

CATEGORY
SIGNAGE

HOOKS FOR HANGING
BASKETS AND DRIED
CLUSTERS, BANANAS OR
BAGGED PRODUCE

±6'-0"

MATERIAL SHOULD
BE DURABLE AND
EASILY CLEANED
(LIKE STAINLESS
STEEL OR TILE)

TIERED DISPLAY
FOR GROWING HERBS,
BINS OF PRODUCE

±3'-0"

NOTE: PROVIDE
DRAINS AND TROUGH
IF PRODUCE IS TO BE
WATERED OR REFRESHED

## "GREEN GROCER" DISPLAY

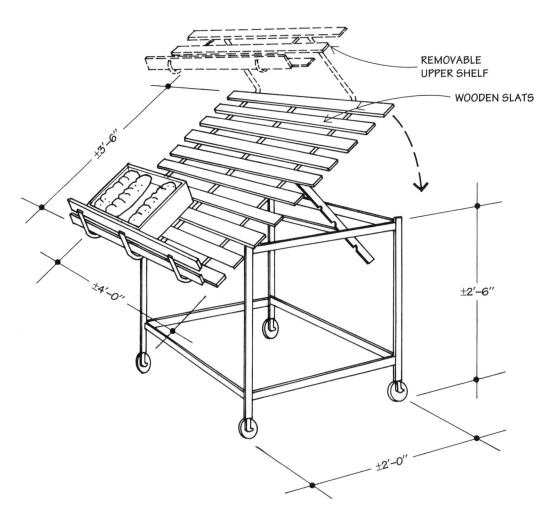

REMOVABLE
UPPER SHELF

WOODEN SLATS

±3'-6"

±4'-0"

±2'-6"

±2'-0"

**ADJUSTABLE DISPLAY**

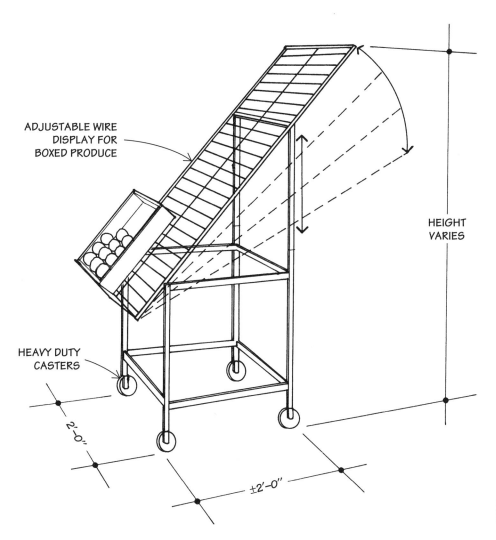

ADJUSTABLE WIRE
DISPLAY FOR
BOXED PRODUCE

HEIGHT
VARIES

HEAVY DUTY
CASTERS

2'-0"

±2'-0"

**ADJUSTABLE WIRE
DISPLAY**

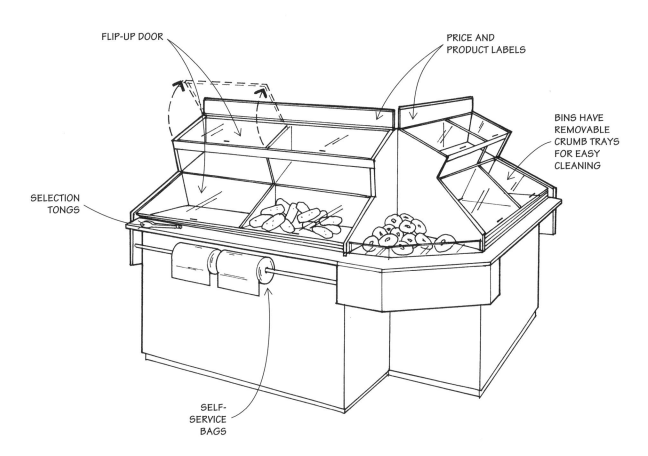

FLIP-UP DOOR

PRICE AND
PRODUCT LABELS

BINS HAVE
REMOVABLE
CRUMB TRAYS
FOR EASY
CLEANING

SELECTION
TONGS

SELF-
SERVICE
BAGS

**TIERED BAKERY DISPLAY**

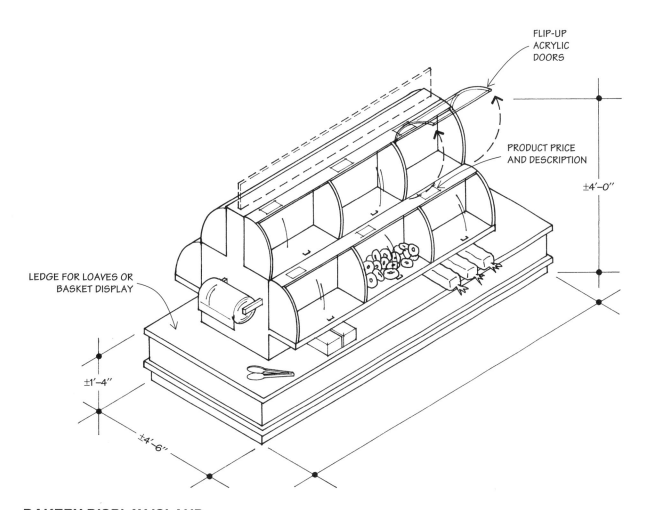

FLIP-UP
ACRYLIC
DOORS

PRODUCT PRICE
AND DESCRIPTION

±4'-0"

LEDGE FOR LOAVES OR
BASKET DISPLAY

±1'-4"

±4'-6"

**BAKERY DISPLAY ISLAND**

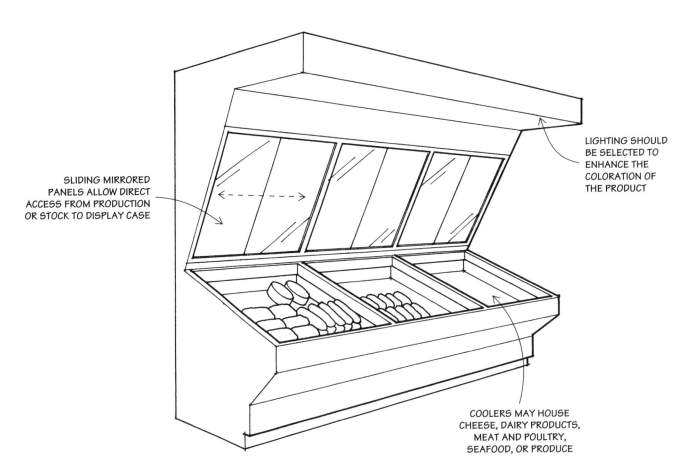

SLIDING MIRRORED
PANELS ALLOW DIRECT
ACCESS FROM PRODUCTION
OR STOCK TO DISPLAY CASE

LIGHTING SHOULD
BE SELECTED TO
ENHANCE THE
COLORATION OF
THE PRODUCT

COOLERS MAY HOUSE
CHEESE, DAIRY PRODUCTS,
MEAT AND POULTRY,
SEAFOOD, OR PRODUCE

**PERIMETER SELF-SERVICE COOLER**

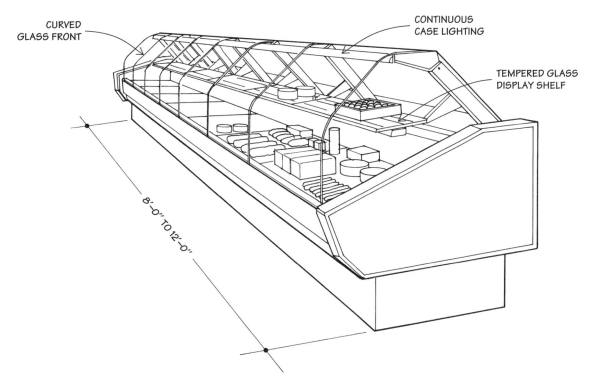

CURVED
GLASS FRONT

CONTINUOUS
CASE LIGHTING

TEMPERED GLASS
DISPLAY SHELF

8'-0" TO 12'-0"

**REFRIGERATED CASE**

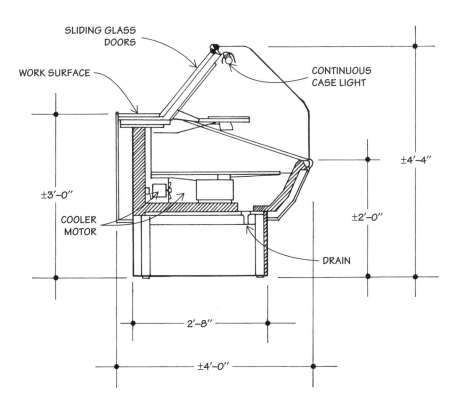

SLIDING GLASS
DOORS

WORK SURFACE

CONTINUOUS
CASE LIGHT

±4'-4"

±3'-0"

±2'-0"

COOLER
MOTOR

DRAIN

2'-8"

±4'-0"

**SECTION THROUGH
REFRIGERATED CASE**

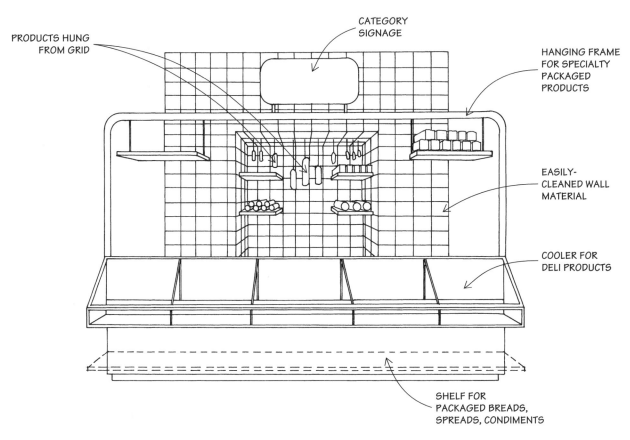

PRODUCTS HUNG
FROM GRID

CATEGORY
SIGNAGE

HANGING FRAME
FOR SPECIALTY
PACKAGED
PRODUCTS

EASILY-
CLEANED WALL
MATERIAL

COOLER FOR
DELI PRODUCTS

SHELF FOR
PACKAGED BREADS,
SPREADS, CONDIMENTS

**FRONT DISPLAY AND MERCHANDISING UNIT**

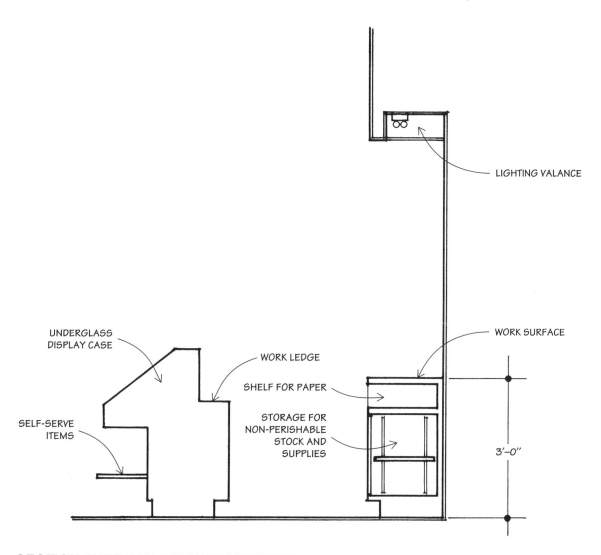

UNDERGLASS
DISPLAY CASE

WORK LEDGE

SHELF FOR PAPER

SELF-SERVE
ITEMS

STORAGE FOR
NON-PERISHABLE
STOCK AND
SUPPLIES

LIGHTING VALANCE

WORK SURFACE

3'-0"

**SECTION THROUGH DELI DEPARTMENT**

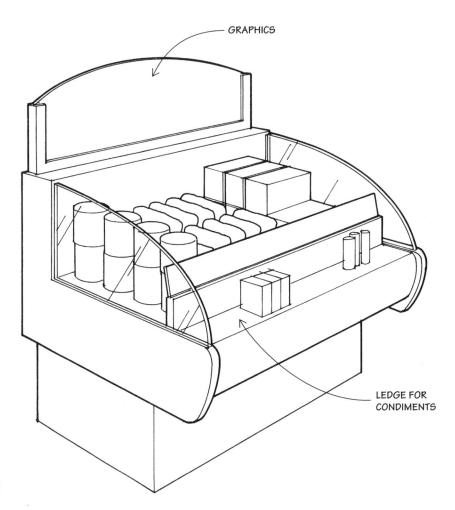

GRAPHICS

LEDGE FOR
CONDIMENTS

**SELF-SERVE DELI COOLER**

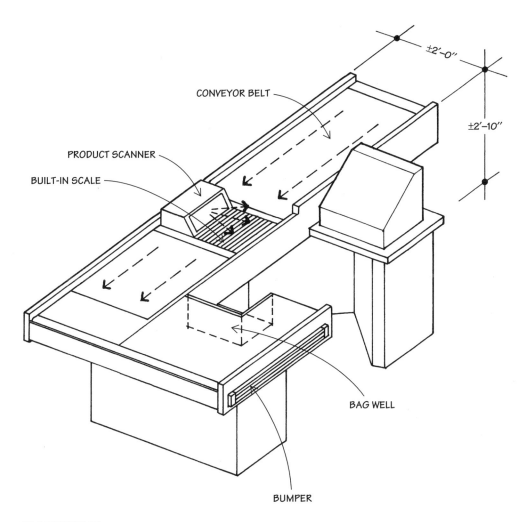

±2'-0"

±2'-10"

CONVEYOR BELT

PRODUCT SCANNER

BUILT-IN SCALE

BAG WELL

BUMPER

## CHECKOUT

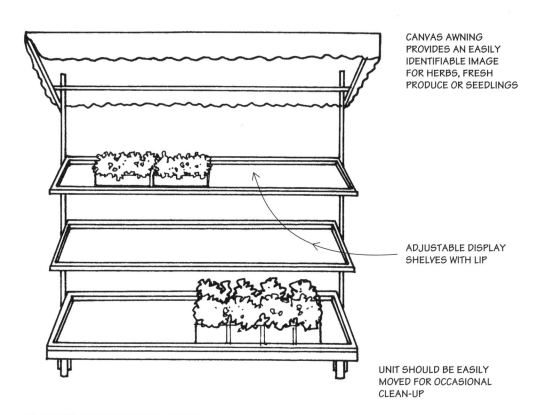

CANVAS AWNING
PROVIDES AN EASILY
IDENTIFIABLE IMAGE
FOR HERBS, FRESH
PRODUCE OR SEEDLINGS

ADJUSTABLE DISPLAY
SHELVES WITH LIP

UNIT SHOULD BE EASILY
MOVED FOR OCCASIONAL
CLEAN-UP

**PLANTS AND HERBS DISPLAY**

# 8

# Convenience
# Stores

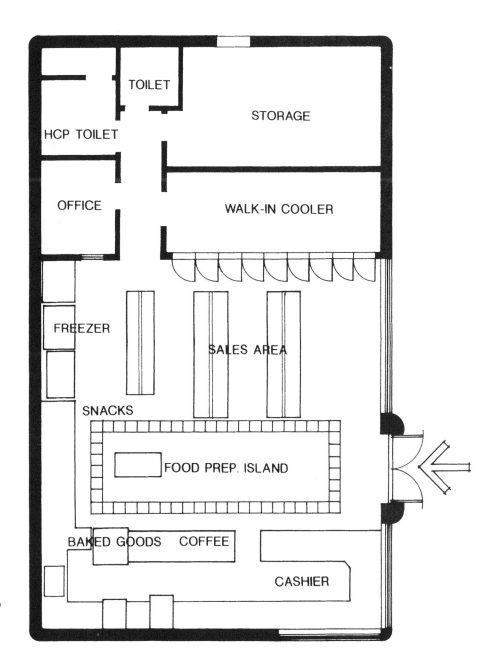

TOILET

STORAGE

HCP TOILET

OFFICE

WALK-IN COOLER

FREEZER

SALES AREA

SNACKS

FOOD PREP. ISLAND

BAKED GOODS    COFFEE

CASHIER

**CONVENIENCE STORE,
PART OF A GASOLINE
SERVICE STATION**

## Tips and Guidelines

1. Category includes units that are:
   - Free-standing.
   - Within a service station.
   - In an apartment house or apartment complex.
2. Sign program should be designed to help customers quickly locate items they need.
3. Refrigerator cases for dairy products and chilled drinks should be placed along a rear wall to pull traffic through the store.
   - Stock area for refills is integrated with refrigerator.
4. Self-service areas are popular.
   - ATM station.
   - Coffee and tea; bagels, muffins, and baked goods; and snacks are popular impulse purchases.
   - Some convenience stores have eating areas.
5. Select materials for cleanability and ease of maintenance.
   - Small staff is responsible for stock and operations.

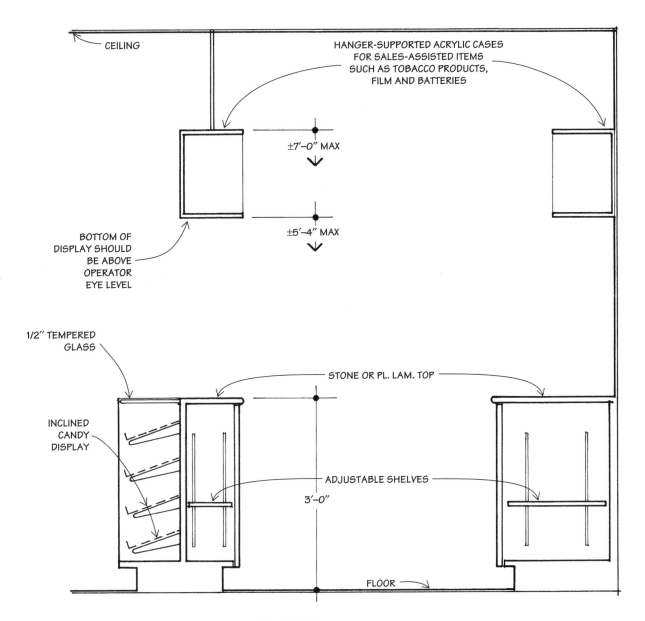

CEILING

HANGER-SUPPORTED ACRYLIC CASES
FOR SALES-ASSISTED ITEMS
SUCH AS TOBACCO PRODUCTS,
FILM AND BATTERIES

±7'-0" MAX

±5'-4" MAX

BOTTOM OF
DISPLAY SHOULD
BE ABOVE
OPERATOR
EYE LEVEL

1/2" TEMPERED
GLASS

STONE OR PL. LAM. TOP

INCLINED
CANDY
DISPLAY

ADJUSTABLE SHELVES

3'-0"

FLOOR

## SECTION THROUGH CASHIER'S COUNTER

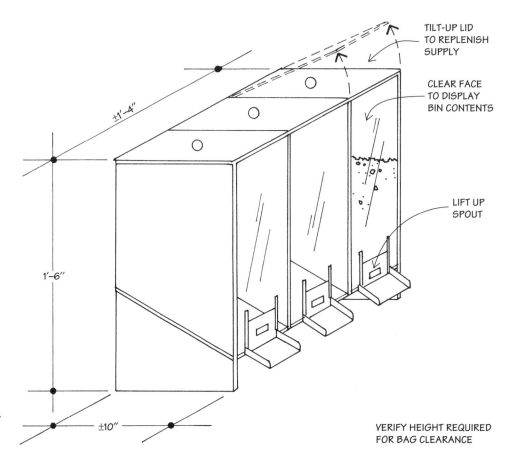

TILT-UP LID
TO REPLENISH
SUPPLY

CLEAR FACE
TO DISPLAY
BIN CONTENTS

LIFT UP
SPOUT

±1'-4"

1'-6"

±10"

**COFFEE AND CANDY
DISPENSER**

VERIFY HEIGHT REQUIRED
FOR BAG CLEARANCE

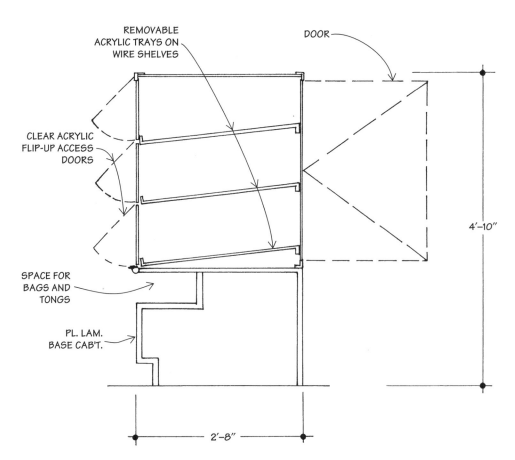

REMOVABLE
ACRYLIC TRAYS ON
WIRE SHELVES

DOOR

CLEAR ACRYLIC
FLIP-UP ACCESS
DOORS

4'-10"

SPACE FOR
BAGS AND
TONGS

PL. LAM.
BASE CAB'T.

**BAKED GOODS
CABINET**

2'-8"

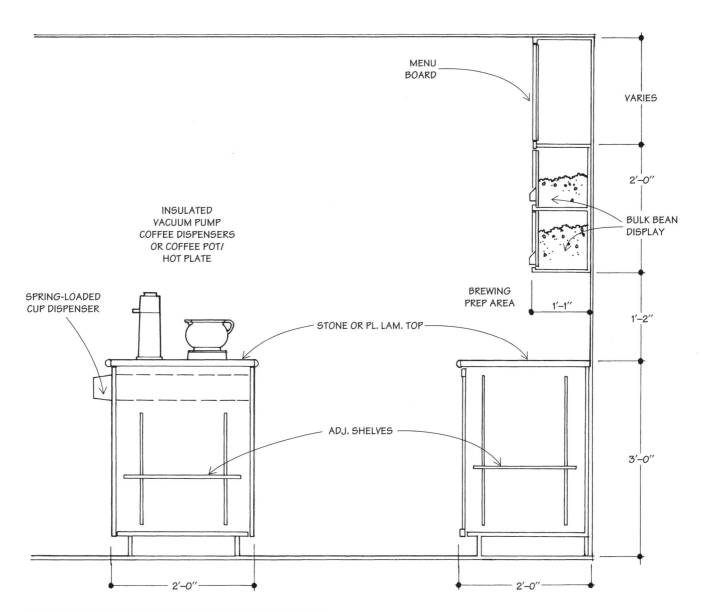

MENU
BOARD

VARIES

2'-0"

INSULATED
VACUUM PUMP
COFFEE DISPENSERS
OR COFFEE POT/
HOT PLATE

BULK BEAN
DISPLAY

SPRING-LOADED
CUP DISPENSER

BREWING
PREP AREA

1'-1"

STONE OR PL. LAM. TOP

1'-2"

ADJ. SHELVES

3'-0"

2'-0"

2'-0"

**SECTION THROUGH COFFEE DEPARTMENT**

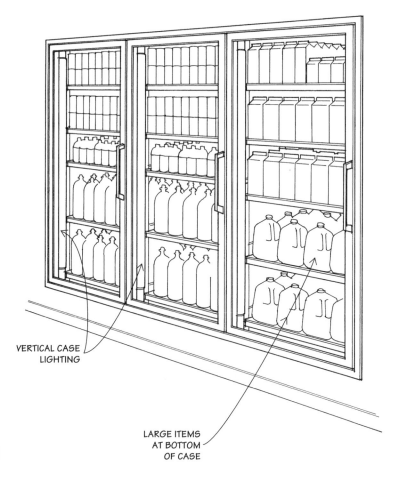

VERTICAL CASE
LIGHTING

LARGE ITEMS
AT BOTTOM
OF CASE

**COOLER ELEVATION**

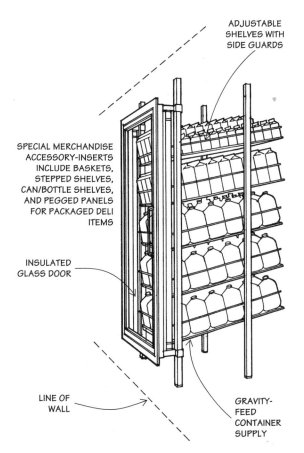

ADJUSTABLE
SHELVES WITH
SIDE GUARDS

SPECIAL MERCHANDISE
ACCESSORY-INSERTS
INCLUDE BASKETS,
STEPPED SHELVES,
CAN/BOTTLE SHELVES,
AND PEGGED PANELS
FOR PACKAGED DELI
ITEMS

INSULATED
GLASS DOOR

LINE OF
WALL

GRAVITY-
FEED
CONTAINER
SUPPLY

**COOLER CROSS-SECTION**

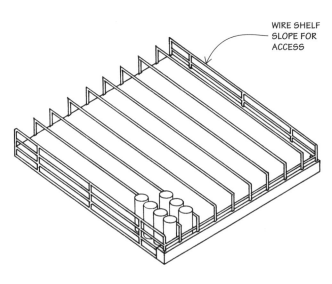

WIRE SHELF
SLOPE FOR
ACCESS

**CAN OR BOTTLE SHELF**

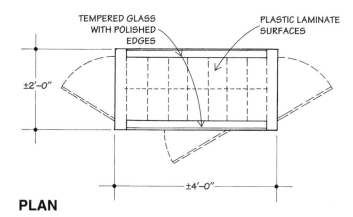

**PLAN**

**CONDIMENT PREPARATION ISLAND**

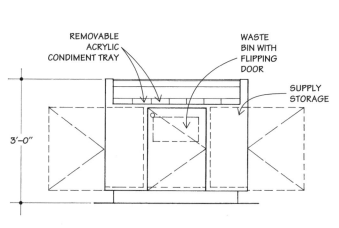

**ELEVATION**

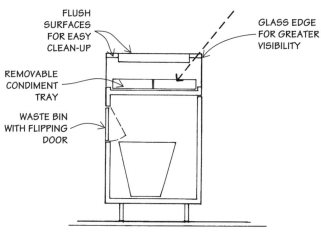

**CROSS-SECTION**

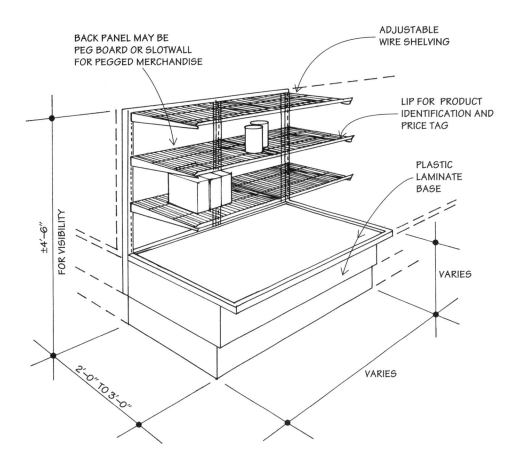

**OPEN-FRONT MERCHANDISER**

# 9

# Housewares
# Stores

STOCK

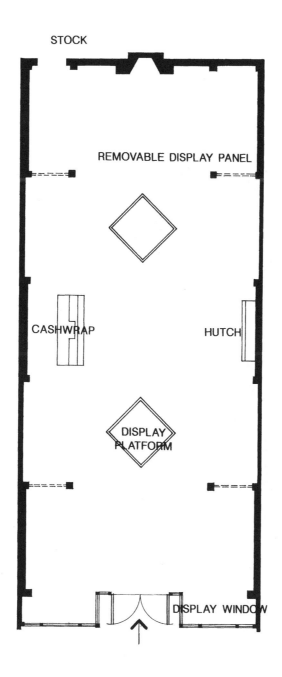

REMOVABLE DISPLAY PANEL

CASHWRAP

HUTCH

DISPLAY
PLATFORM

DISPLAY WINDOW

**HOUSEWARES STORE
LOCATED IN A
SHOPPING MALL**

## Tips and Guidelines

1. Category includes home furnishings and accessories stores.

   - Merchandise ranges from small kitchen and bath appliances to tables, chairs, stools, etc.

2. Selling floor should offer customers the opportunity to view merchandise in mini-environments.

   - Create viewing perspectives in the plan.

   - Use open plan, with variations on basic racetrack or sawtooth layouts.

   - Allow for space and illumination for vignettes featuring place settings, glassware, table linens, bedding, towels.

3. Materials and finishes should have a residential quality.

   - Provide for flexibility for staff to change floor and window displays.

   - Consider seasonal and holiday needs.

4. Attractively boxed merchandise can be stacked to create free-standing island displays.

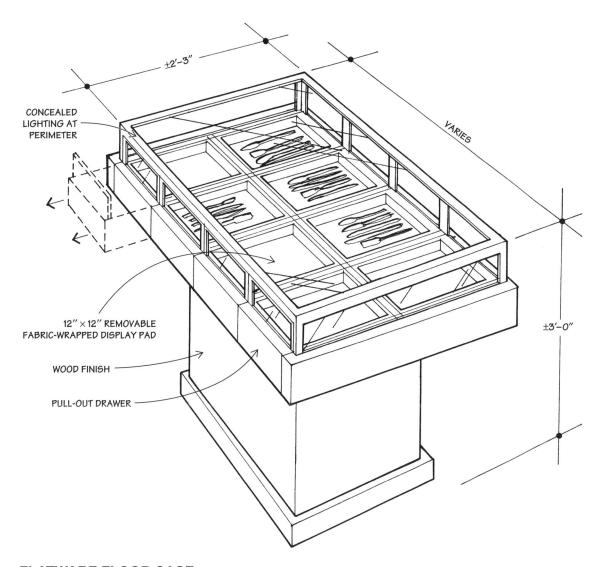

CONCEALED
LIGHTING AT
PERIMETER

±2'-3"

VARIES

±3'-0"

12" × 12" REMOVABLE
FABRIC-WRAPPED DISPLAY PAD

WOOD FINISH

PULL-OUT DRAWER

## FLATWARE FLOOR CASE

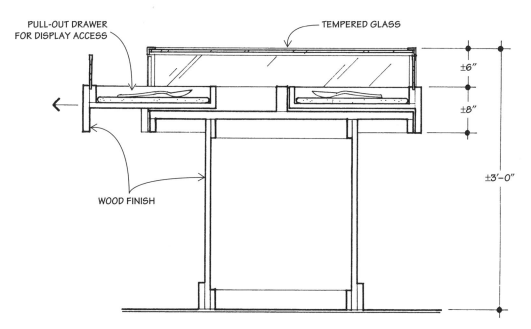

PULL-OUT DRAWER
FOR DISPLAY ACCESS

TEMPERED GLASS

±6"

±8"

±3'-0"

WOOD FINISH

**FLATWARE FLOOR
CASE SECTION**

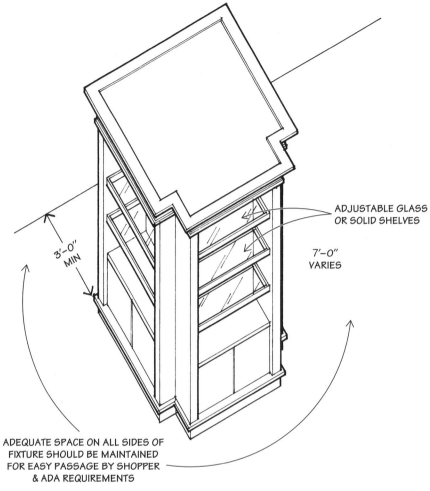

ADJUSTABLE GLASS
OR SOLID SHELVES

3'-0"
MIN

7'-0"
VARIES

ADEQUATE SPACE ON ALL SIDES OF
FIXTURE SHOULD BE MAINTAINED
FOR EASY PASSAGE BY SHOPPER
& ADA REQUIREMENTS

## HOUSEWARES DISPLAY TOWER

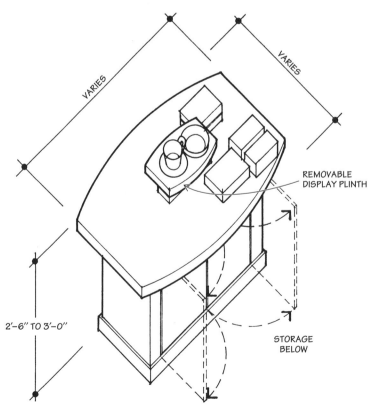

VARIES

VARIES

REMOVABLE
DISPLAY PLINTH

2'-6" TO 3'-0"

STORAGE
BELOW

## HOUSEWARES DISPLAY AND STORAGE BASE

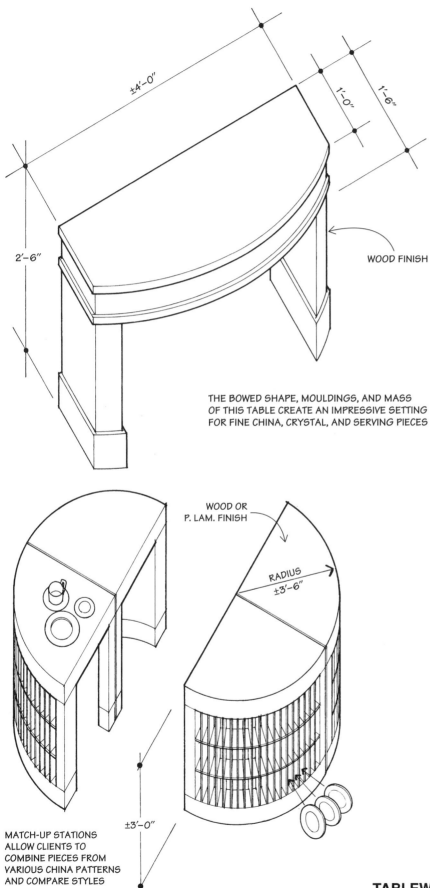

±4'-0"

1'-0"

1'-6"

2'-6"

WOOD FINISH

THE BOWED SHAPE, MOULDINGS, AND MASS
OF THIS TABLE CREATE AN IMPRESSIVE SETTING
FOR FINE CHINA, CRYSTAL, AND SERVING PIECES

**BOWED PRESENTATION
TABLE**

WOOD OR
P. LAM. FINISH

RADIUS
±3'-6"

±3'-0"

MATCH-UP STATIONS
ALLOW CLIENTS TO
COMBINE PIECES FROM
VARIOUS CHINA PATTERNS
AND COMPARE STYLES

**TABLEWARE MATCH-UP STATION**

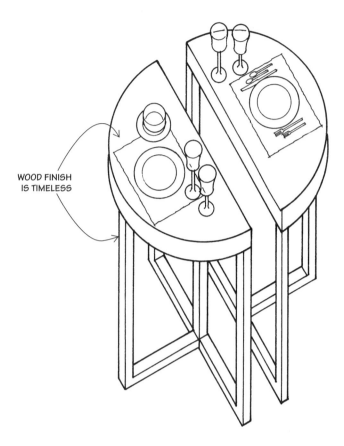

WOOD FINISH
IS TIMELESS

**HALF-ROUND DISPLAY TABLES**

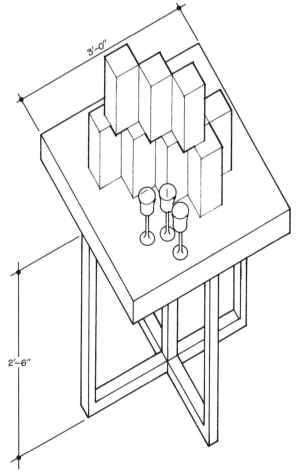

3'-0"

2'-6"

**SQUARE DISPLAY TABLE**

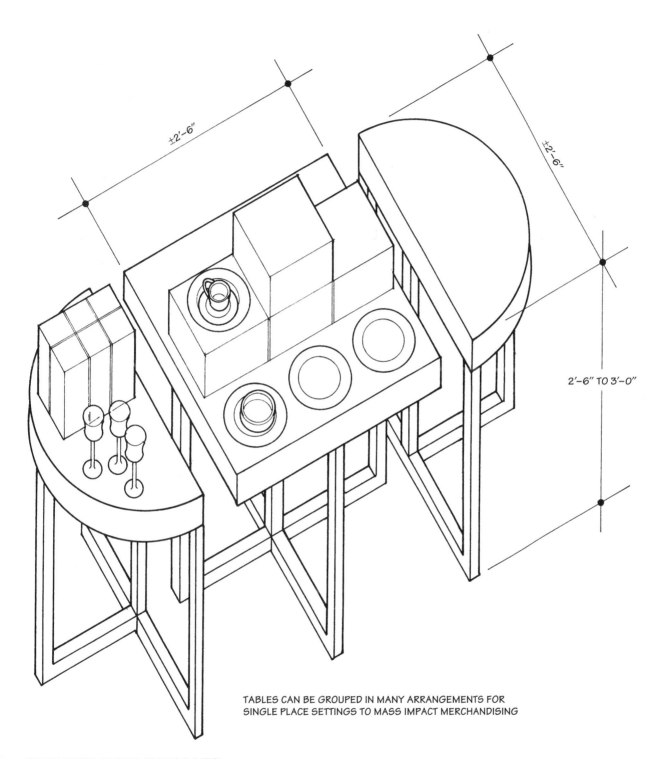

±2'-6"

±2'-6"

2'-6" TO 3'-0"

TABLES CAN BE GROUPED IN MANY ARRANGEMENTS FOR
SINGLE PLACE SETTINGS TO MASS IMPACT MERCHANDISING

**GROUPED DISPLAY TABLES**

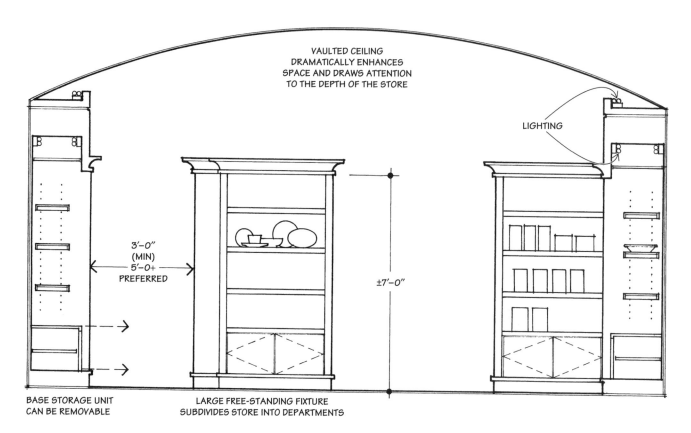

VAULTED CEILING
DRAMATICALLY ENHANCES
SPACE AND DRAWS ATTENTION
TO THE DEPTH OF THE STORE

LIGHTING

3'-0"
(MIN)
5'-0+
PREFERRED

±7'-0"

BASE STORAGE UNIT
CAN BE REMOVABLE

LARGE FREE-STANDING FIXTURE
SUBDIVIDES STORE INTO DEPARTMENTS

## STORE CROSS-SECTION

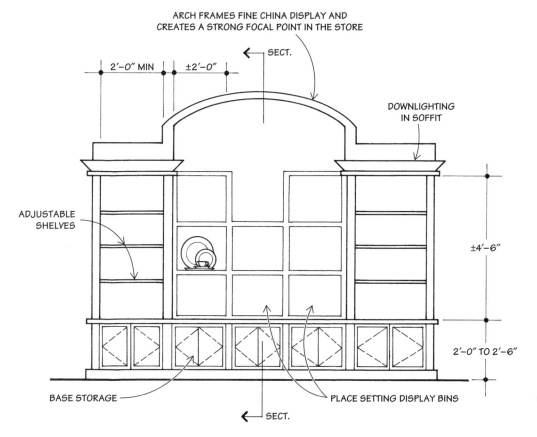

ARCH FRAMES FINE CHINA DISPLAY AND
CREATES A STRONG FOCAL POINT IN THE STORE

SECT.

2'-0" MIN    ±2'-0"

DOWNLIGHTING
IN SOFFIT

ADJUSTABLE
SHELVES

±4'-6"

2'-0" TO 2'-6"

BASE STORAGE

PLACE SETTING DISPLAY BINS

SECT.

**TABLEWARE
DISPLAY UNIT**

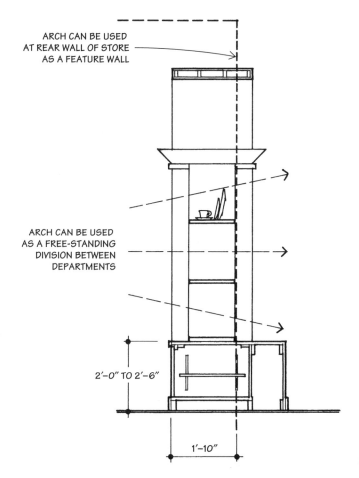

ARCH CAN BE USED
AT REAR WALL OF STORE
AS A FEATURE WALL

ARCH CAN BE USED
AS A FREE-STANDING
DIVISION BETWEEN
DEPARTMENTS

2'-0" TO 2'-6"

1'-10"

**SECTION THROUGH TABLEWARE DISPLAY**

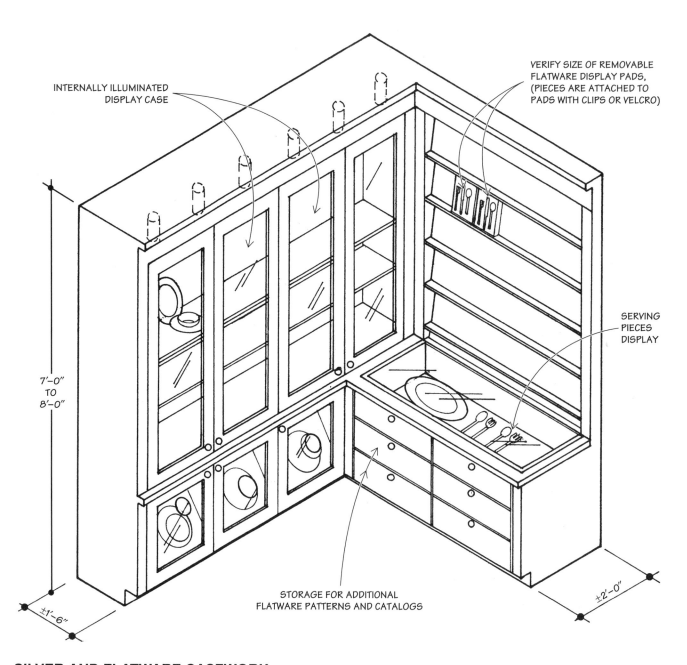

INTERNALLY ILLUMINATED
DISPLAY CASE

VERIFY SIZE OF REMOVABLE
FLATWARE DISPLAY PADS,
(PIECES ARE ATTACHED TO
PADS WITH CLIPS OR VELCRO)

SERVING
PIECES
DISPLAY

7'-0"
TO
8'-0"

±1'-6"

STORAGE FOR ADDITIONAL
FLATWARE PATTERNS AND CATALOGS

±2'-0"

## SILVER AND FLATWARE CASEWORK

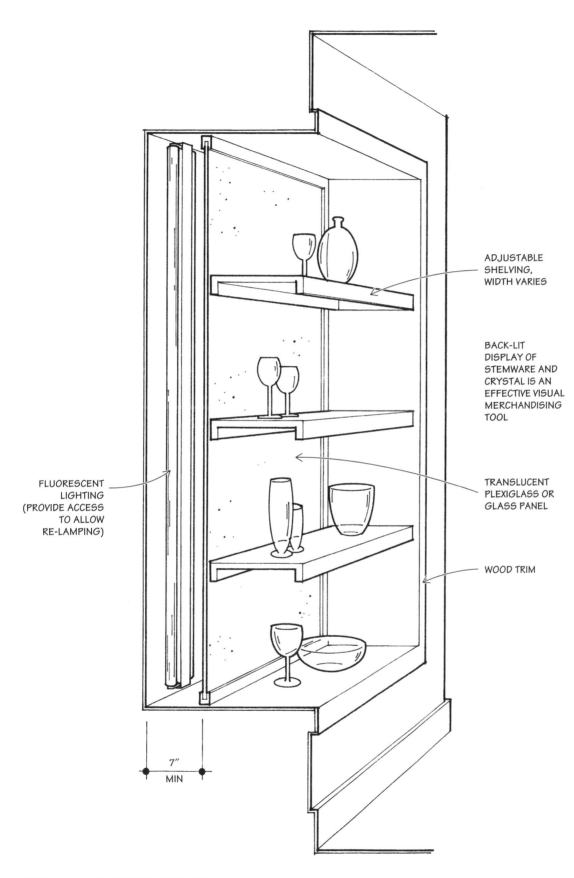

ADJUSTABLE
SHELVING,
WIDTH VARIES

BACK-LIT
DISPLAY OF
STEMWARE AND
CRYSTAL IS AN
EFFECTIVE VISUAL
MERCHANDISING
TOOL

TRANSLUCENT
PLEXIGLASS OR
GLASS PANEL

WOOD TRIM

FLUORESCENT
LIGHTING
(PROVIDE ACCESS
TO ALLOW
RE-LAMPING)

7"
MIN

**TYPICAL HOUSEWARES WALL**

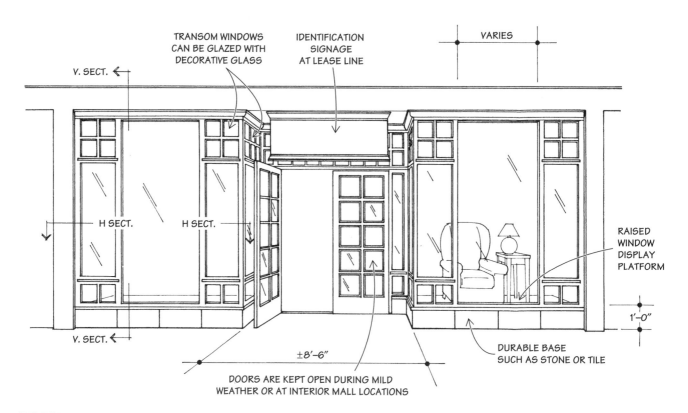

TRANSOM WINDOWS
CAN BE GLAZED WITH
DECORATIVE GLASS

IDENTIFICATION
SIGNAGE
AT LEASE LINE

VARIES

V. SECT.

H SECT.    H SECT.

V. SECT.

±8'-6"

DOORS ARE KEPT OPEN DURING MILD
WEATHER OR AT INTERIOR MALL LOCATIONS

RAISED
WINDOW
DISPLAY
PLATFORM

1'-0"

DURABLE BASE
SUCH AS STONE OR TILE

**POSSIBLE HOUSEWARES FRONT
ELEVATION**

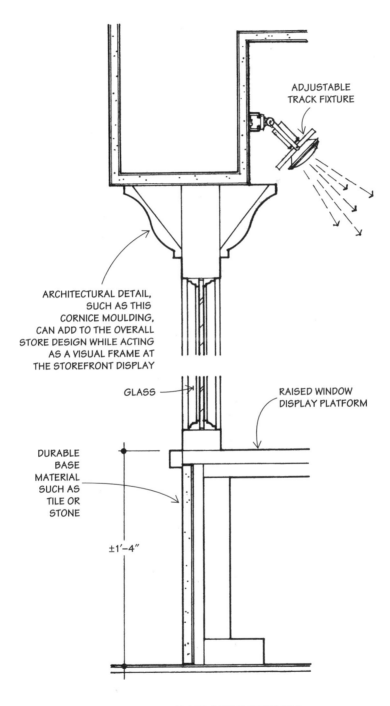

ADJUSTABLE
TRACK FIXTURE

ARCHITECTURAL DETAIL,
SUCH AS THIS
CORNICE MOULDING,
CAN ADD TO THE OVERALL
STORE DESIGN WHILE ACTING
AS A VISUAL FRAME AT
THE STOREFRONT DISPLAY

GLASS

RAISED WINDOW
DISPLAY PLATFORM

DURABLE
BASE
MATERIAL
SUCH AS
TILE OR
STONE

±1'−4"

**VERTICAL WINDOW SECTION**

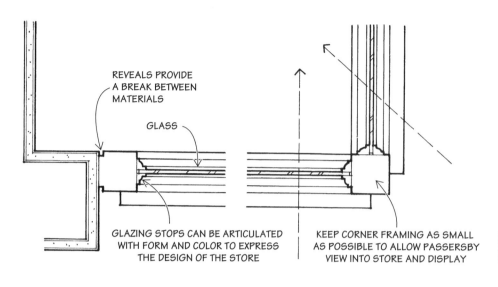

REVEALS PROVIDE A BREAK BETWEEN MATERIALS

GLASS

GLAZING STOPS CAN BE ARTICULATED WITH FORM AND COLOR TO EXPRESS THE DESIGN OF THE STORE

KEEP CORNER FRAMING AS SMALL AS POSSIBLE TO ALLOW PASSERSBY VIEW INTO STORE AND DISPLAY

**HORIZONTAL WINDOW MOLDING SECTION**

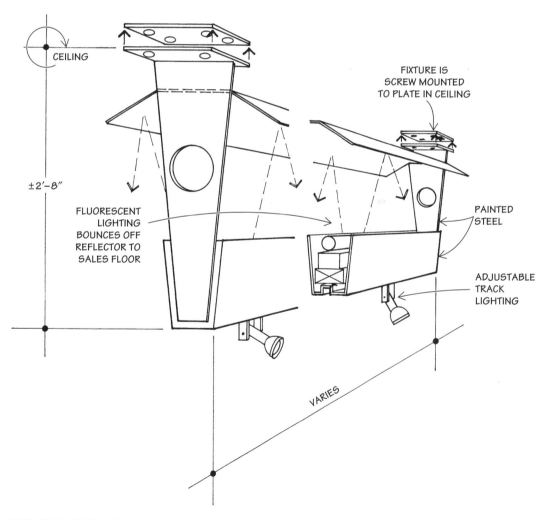

CEILING

±2'-8"

FLUORESCENT LIGHTING BOUNCES OFF REFLECTOR TO SALES FLOOR

FIXTURE IS SCREW MOUNTED TO PLATE IN CEILING

PAINTED STEEL

ADJUSTABLE TRACK LIGHTING

VARIES

**CEILING TROUGH FOR AMBIENT AND DISPLAY LIGHTING**

# Bookstores

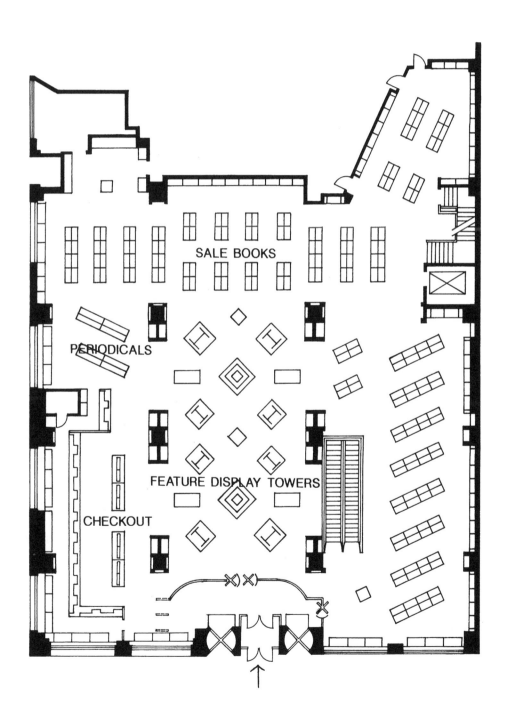

SALE BOOKS

PERIODICALS

FEATURE DISPLAY TOWERS

CHECKOUT

**BOOKSTORE IN AN URBAN LOCATION. STORE OCCUPIES GROUND FLOOR, BALCONY, AND LOWER LEVEL**

10

## Tips and Guidelines

1. Retail book outlets range from small neighborhood shops to "category killers" of 100,000+ titles.

2. In addition to the cashwrap station, provide for information and special-order areas containing one or more computer terminals.

3. Provide racks and displays for periodicals.

   ▪ Larger bookstores have an extensive selection of domestic and foreign magazines.

4. Provide spaces for:

   ▪ Seating corners for browsers.

   ▪ Children's area for reading, presentations.

   ▪ Events area, for signings, readings, speakers.

   ▪ Cafe.

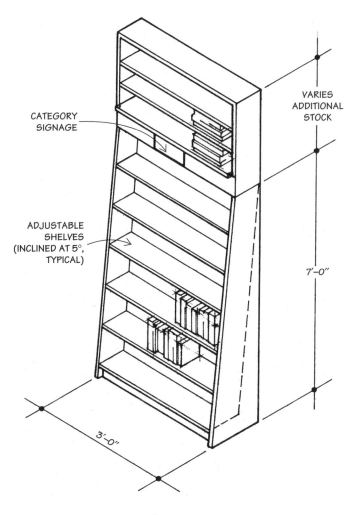

CATEGORY
SIGNAGE

ADJUSTABLE
SHELVES
(INCLINED AT 5°,
TYPICAL)

VARIES
ADDITIONAL
STOCK

7'-0"

3'-0"

**TYPICAL BOOKSHELVING UNIT**

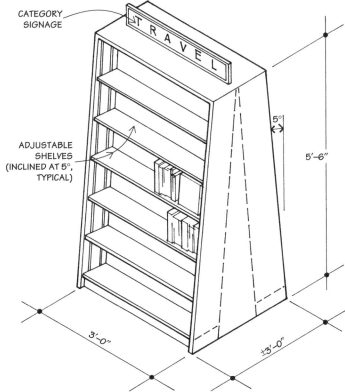

CATEGORY
SIGNAGE

T R A V E L

ADJUSTABLE
SHELVES
(INCLINED AT 5°,
TYPICAL)

5°

5'-6"

3'-0"

±3'-0"

**BACK-TO-BACK SHELVING**

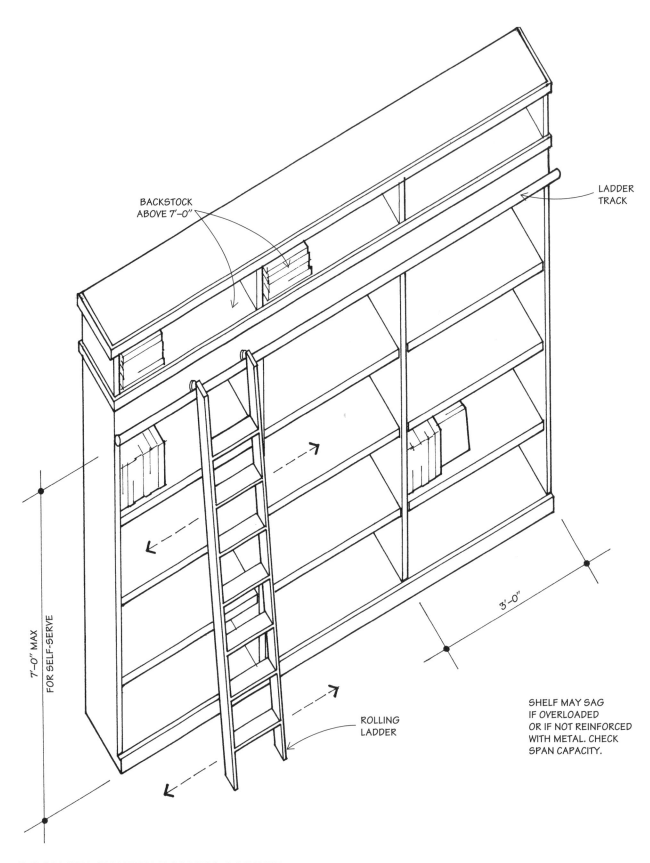

BACKSTOCK
ABOVE 7'-0"

LADDER
TRACK

7'-0" MAX
FOR SELF-SERVE

3'-0"

ROLLING
LADDER

SHELF MAY SAG
IF OVERLOADED
OR IF NOT REINFORCED
WITH METAL. CHECK
SPAN CAPACITY.

**BOOK STACK WITH ROLLING LADDER**

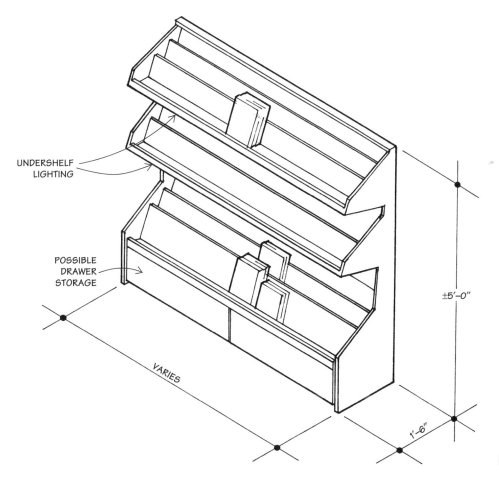

UNDERSHELF
LIGHTING

POSSIBLE
DRAWER
STORAGE

±5'-0"

VARIES

1'-6"

**MAGAZINE RACK**

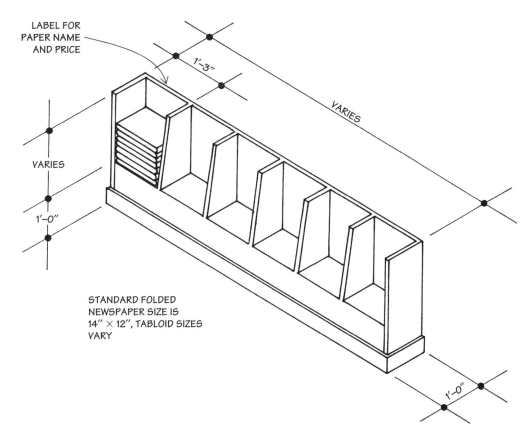

LABEL FOR
PAPER NAME
AND PRICE

1'-3"

VARIES

VARIES

1'-0"

STANDARD FOLDED
NEWSPAPER SIZE IS
14" × 12", TABLOID SIZES
VARY

1'-0"

**FLOOR-MOUNTED
NEWS UNIT**

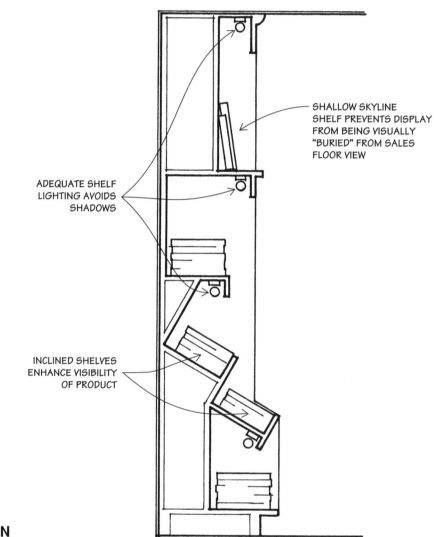

SHALLOW SKYLINE
SHELF PREVENTS DISPLAY
FROM BEING VISUALLY
"BURIED" FROM SALES
FLOOR VIEW

ADEQUATE SHELF
LIGHTING AVOIDS
SHADOWS

INCLINED SHELVES
ENHANCE VISIBILITY
OF PRODUCT

**CROSS-SECTION**

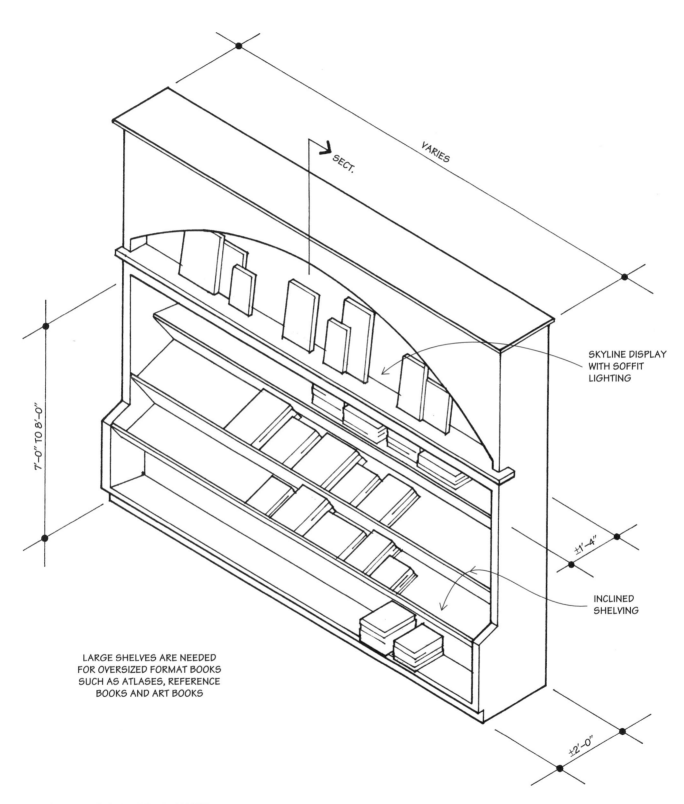

VARIES

SECT.

SKYLINE DISPLAY
WITH SOFFIT
LIGHTING

7'-0" TO 8'-0"

±1'-4"

INCLINED
SHELVING

LARGE SHELVES ARE NEEDED
FOR OVERSIZED FORMAT BOOKS
SUCH AS ATLASES, REFERENCE
BOOKS AND ART BOOKS

±2'-0"

## SPECIAL BOOK WALL UNIT

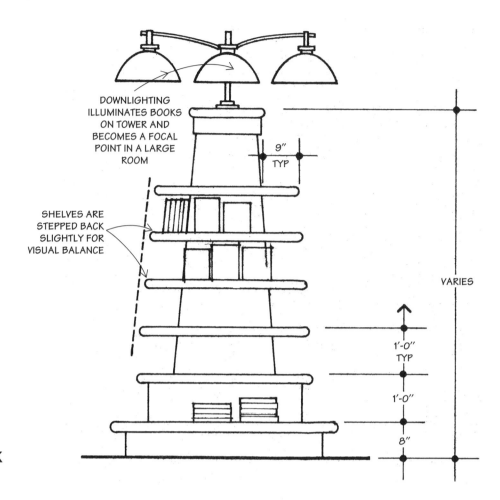

DOWNLIGHTING
ILLUMINATES BOOKS
ON TOWER AND
BECOMES A FOCAL
POINT IN A LARGE
ROOM

9"
TYP

SHELVES ARE
STEPPED BACK
SLIGHTLY FOR
VISUAL BALANCE

VARIES

1'-0"
TYP

1'-0"

8"

**FLOOR ISLAND BOOK
FIXTURE: ELEVATION**

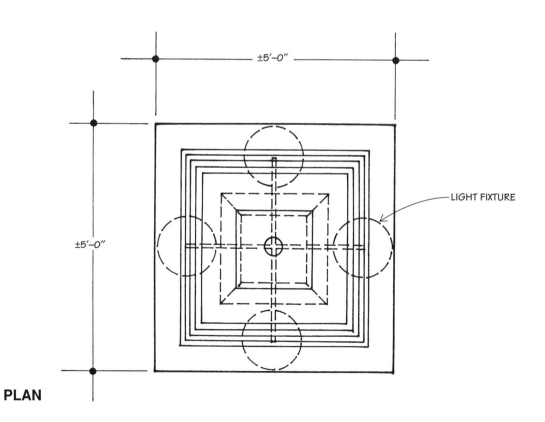

±5'-0"

±5'-0"

LIGHT FIXTURE

**PLAN**

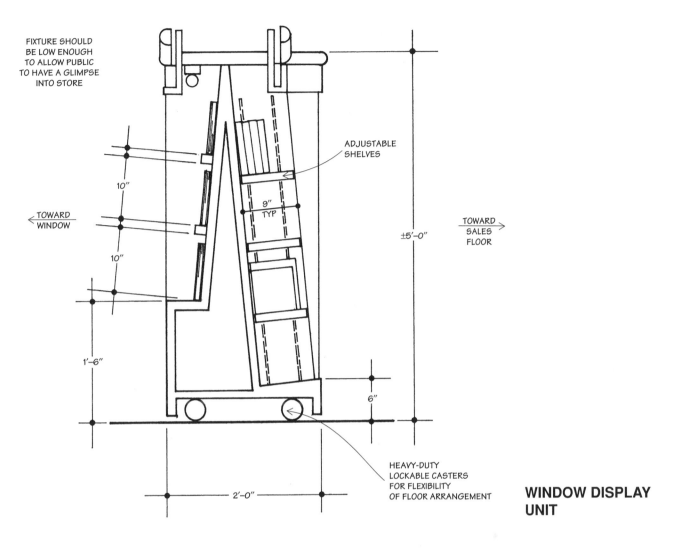

FIXTURE SHOULD
BE LOW ENOUGH
TO ALLOW PUBLIC
TO HAVE A GLIMPSE
INTO STORE

ADJUSTABLE
SHELVES

TOWARD
WINDOW

10"

9"
TYP

10"

TOWARD
SALES
FLOOR

±5'-0"

1'-6"

6"

HEAVY-DUTY
LOCKABLE CASTERS
FOR FLEXIBILITY
OF FLOOR ARRANGEMENT

2'-0"

**WINDOW DISPLAY
UNIT**

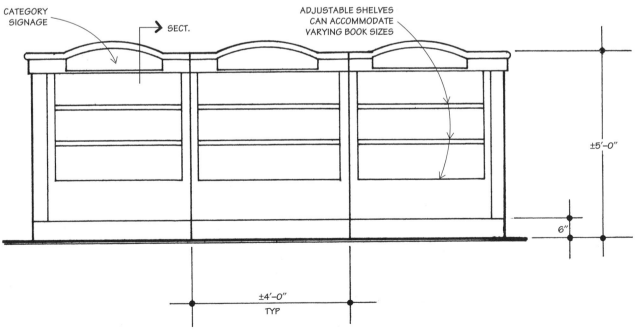

CATEGORY
SIGNAGE

SECT.

ADJUSTABLE SHELVES
CAN ACCOMMODATE
VARYING BOOK SIZES

±5'-0"

6"

±4'-0"
TYP

**WINDOW DISPLAY UNIT VIEWED FROM SALES
FLOOR**

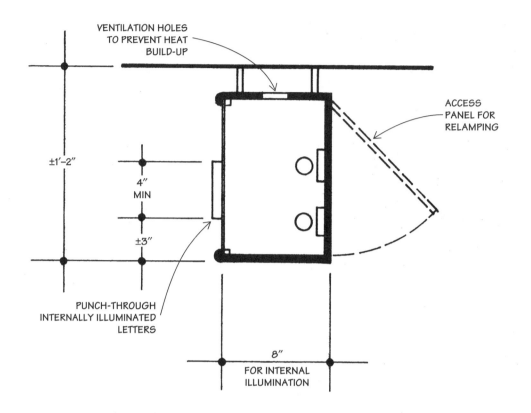

VENTILATION HOLES
TO PREVENT HEAT
BUILD-UP

ACCESS
PANEL FOR
RELAMPING

±1'–2"

4"
MIN

±3"

PUNCH-THROUGH
INTERNALLY ILLUMINATED
LETTERS

8"
FOR INTERNAL
ILLUMINATION

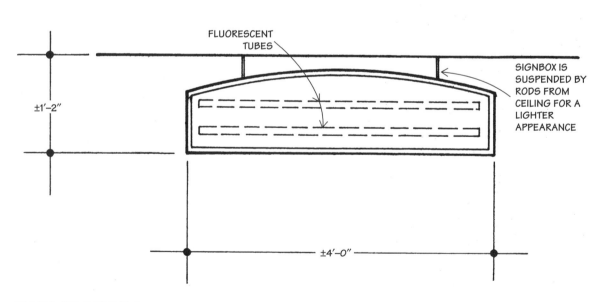

FLUORESCENT
TUBES

SIGNBOX IS
SUSPENDED BY
RODS FROM
CEILING FOR A
LIGHTER
APPEARANCE

±1'–2"

±4'–0"

**SIGNAGE DETAILS**

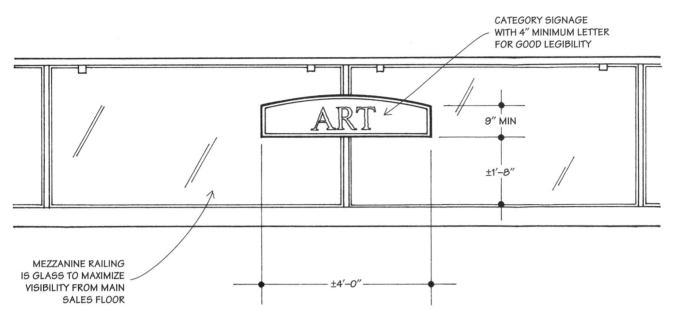

CATEGORY SIGNAGE
WITH 4" MINIMUM LETTER
FOR GOOD LEGIBILITY

ART

9" MIN

±1'–8"

MEZZANINE RAILING
IS GLASS TO MAXIMIZE
VISIBILITY FROM MAIN
SALES FLOOR

±4'–0"

## SIGN CONSIDERATION

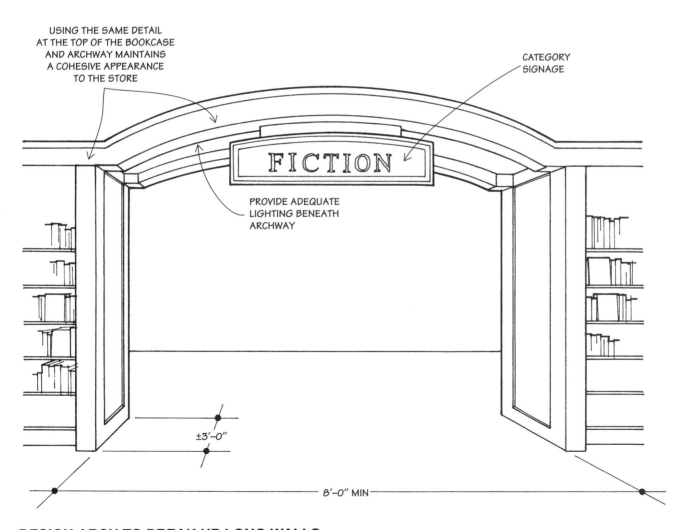

USING THE SAME DETAIL
AT THE TOP OF THE BOOKCASE
AND ARCHWAY MAINTAINS
A COHESIVE APPEARANCE
TO THE STORE

CATEGORY
SIGNAGE

FICTION

PROVIDE ADEQUATE
LIGHTING BENEATH
ARCHWAY

±3'–0"

8'–0" MIN

## DESIGN ARCH TO BREAK UP LONG WALLS

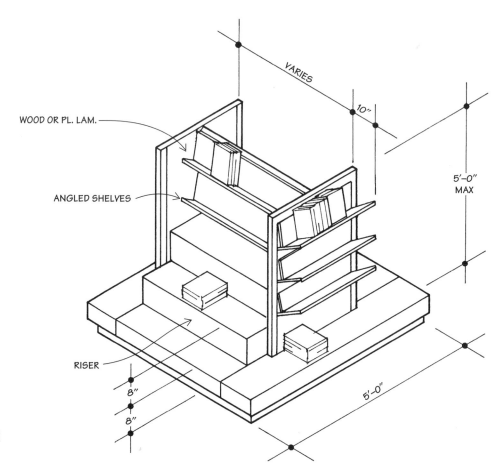

VARIES

10"

5'-0"
MAX

WOOD OR PL. LAM.

ANGLED SHELVES

RISER

8"

8"

5'-0"

**FOUR-SIDED FLOOR
BOOK UNIT**

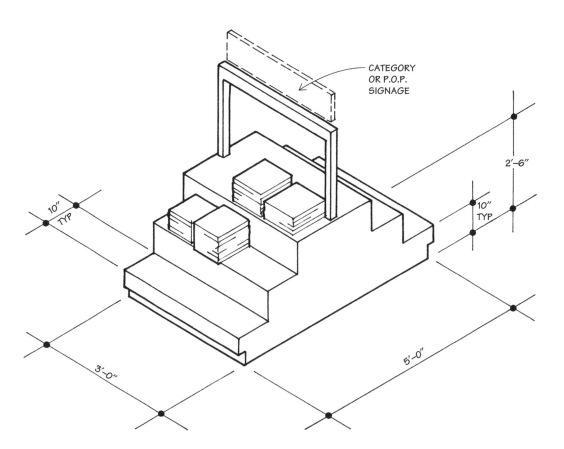

CATEGORY
OR P.O.P.
SIGNAGE

2'-6"

10"
TYP

10"
TYP

3'-0"

5'-0"

**STEPPED BOOK
DISPLAY UNIT**

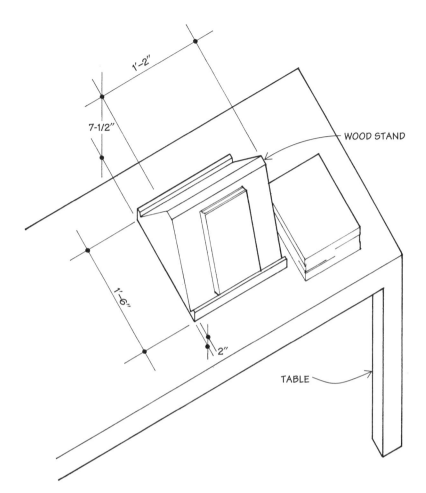

1'-2"

7-1/2"

WOOD STAND

1'-6"

2"

TABLE

**BOOK STAND**

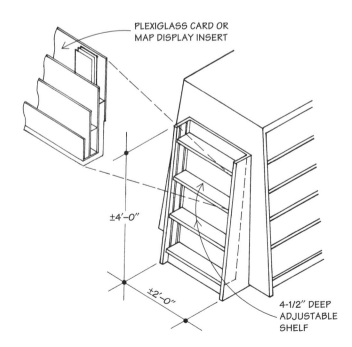

PLEXIGLASS CARD OR
MAP DISPLAY INSERT

±4'-0"

±2'-0"

4-1/2" DEEP
ADJUSTABLE
SHELF

**END-CAP FOR BOOK OR CARD DISPLAY**

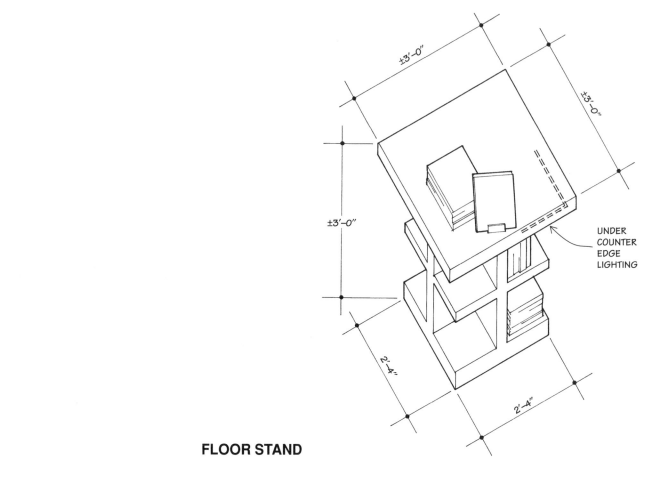

±3'-0"

±3'-0"

±3'-0"

UNDER
COUNTER
EDGE
LIGHTING

2'-4"

2'-4"

**FLOOR STAND**

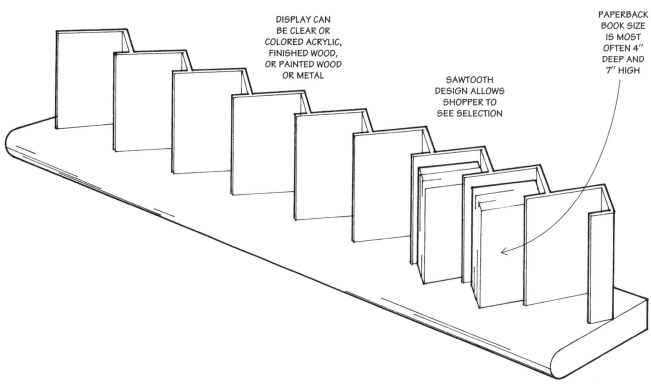

DISPLAY CAN
BE CLEAR OR
COLORED ACRYLIC,
FINISHED WOOD,
OR PAINTED WOOD
OR METAL

SAWTOOTH
DESIGN ALLOWS
SHOPPER TO
SEE SELECTION

PAPERBACK
BOOK SIZE
IS MOST
OFTEN 4"
DEEP AND
7" HIGH

**PARTIAL FACE-FRONT PAPERBACK SHELF**

# 11

# Audio/Video and Computer Stores

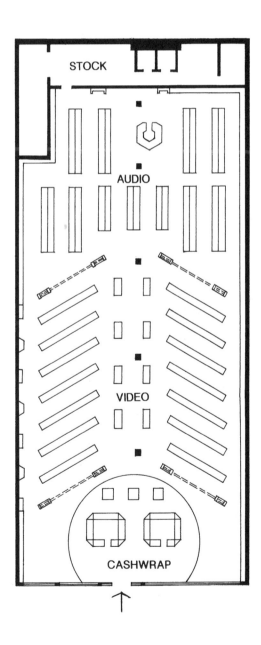

STOCK

AUDIO

VIDEO

CASHWRAP

**AUDIO/VIDEO CHAIN STORE IN A STRIP SHOPPING CENTER**

## Tips and Guidelines

1. Category includes retail stores selling a variety of consumer and business electronic equipment.

   - Can be positioned as a high-end or as a volume store.
   - Includes stores or departments handling tapes, CDs, and videos.

2. Merchandise can be interactive.

   - Customers can try out the equipment themselves at kiosks or wall-mounted displays.
   - Service-oriented stores can have listening rooms for a/v customers or conference areas for computer shoppers.

3. Ambience should be lively, contemporary.

   - An optional design theme for high-end stores can include more traditional lighting, color palette, and materials.

4. Graphics can extend image promoted by advertising and packaging.

   - Directional graphics should permit staff to add new products and merchandise locations.

5. Stores with video rental operations require appropriate shelving, check-out, and check-in facilities.

6. Special security measures required to control theft of small, pocketable items.

   - Electronic scanners, alarms, and other devices.

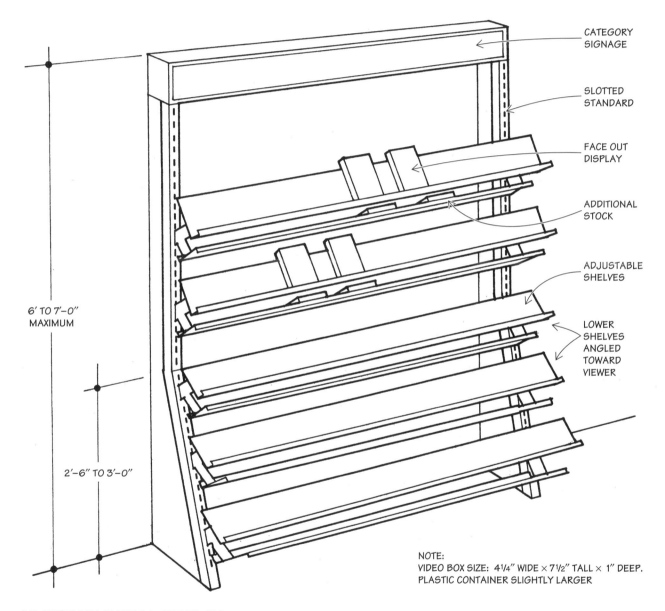

CATEGORY
SIGNAGE

SLOTTED
STANDARD

FACE OUT
DISPLAY

ADDITIONAL
STOCK

ADJUSTABLE
SHELVES

LOWER
SHELVES
ANGLED
TOWARD
VIEWER

6' TO 7'-0"
MAXIMUM

2'-6" TO 3'-0"

NOTE:
VIDEO BOX SIZE: 4¼" WIDE × 7½" TALL × 1" DEEP.
PLASTIC CONTAINER SLIGHTLY LARGER

## ADJUSTABLE WALL DISPLAY

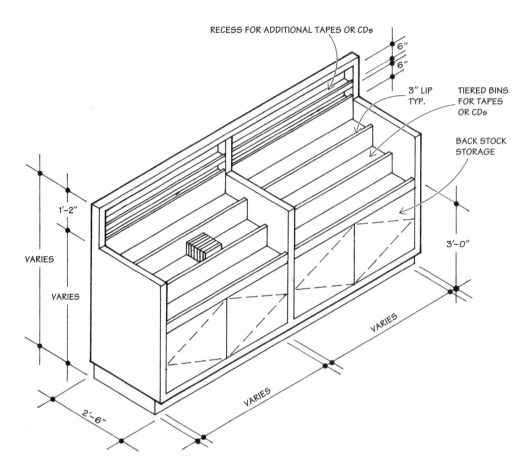

RECESS FOR ADDITIONAL TAPES OR CDs

6"
6"

3" LIP TYP.

TIERED BINS FOR TAPES OR CDs

BACK STOCK STORAGE

1'-2"

VARIES

VARIES

3'-0"

VARIES

VARIES

2'-6"

**AUDIO/VIDEO DISPLAY MODULE**

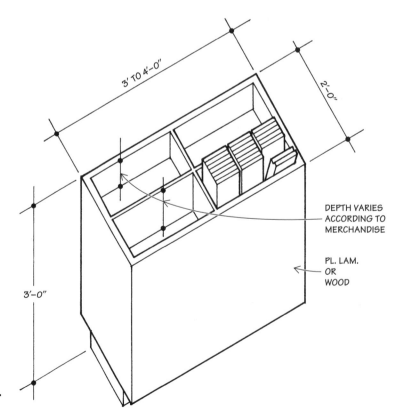

3' TO 4'-0"

2'-0"

DEPTH VARIES ACCORDING TO MERCHANDISE

PL. LAM. OR WOOD

3'-0"

**TWO-SIDED FLOOR UNIT**

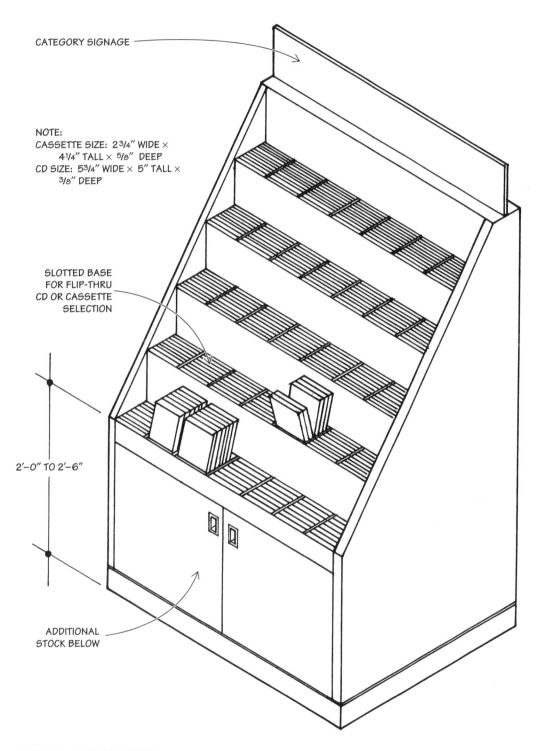

CATEGORY SIGNAGE

NOTE:
CASSETTE SIZE:  2 3/4″ WIDE ×
    4 1/4″ TALL × 5/8″  DEEP
CD SIZE:  5 3/4″ WIDE × 5″ TALL ×
    3/8″ DEEP

SLOTTED BASE
FOR FLIP-THRU
CD OR CASSETTE
SELECTION

2′–0″ TO 2′–6″

ADDITIONAL
STOCK BELOW

**TIERED AUDIO UNIT**

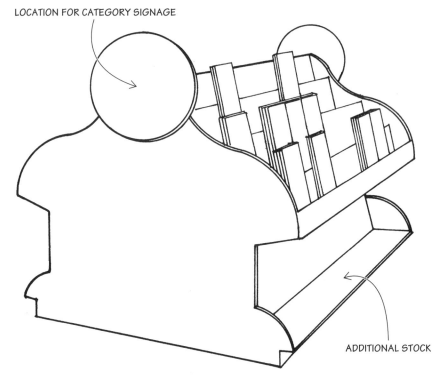

LOCATION FOR CATEGORY SIGNAGE

ADDITIONAL STOCK

**TWO-SIDED AUDIO/VIDEO
MERCHANDISER**

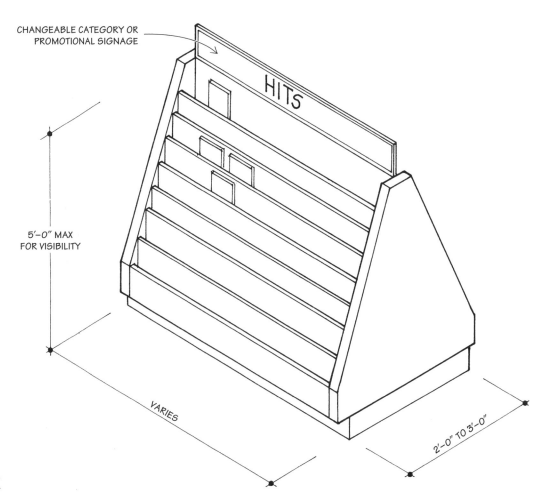

CHANGEABLE CATEGORY OR
PROMOTIONAL SIGNAGE

HITS

5'-0" MAX
FOR VISIBILITY

VARIES

2'-0" TO 3'-0"

**AUDIO/VIDEO
BACK-TO-BACK**

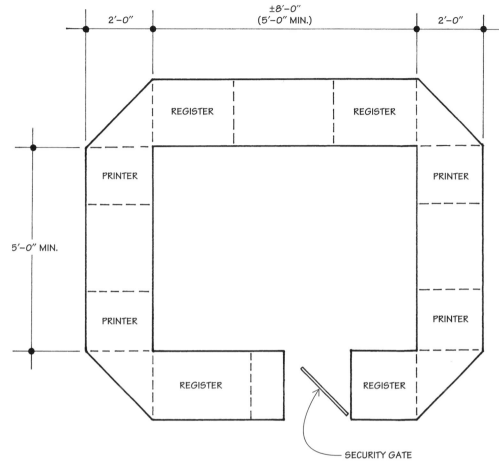

2'-0"

±8'-0"
(5'-0" MIN.)

2'-0"

REGISTER    REGISTER

PRINTER    PRINTER

5'-0" MIN.

PRINTER    PRINTER

REGISTER    REGISTER

SECURITY GATE

VERIFY REGISTER SIZE, POWER AND PHONE REQUIREMENTS

**CASHWRAP PLAN**

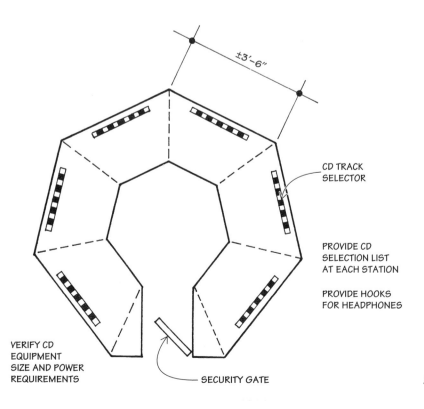

±3'-6"

CD TRACK
SELECTOR

PROVIDE CD
SELECTION LIST
AT EACH STATION

PROVIDE HOOKS
FOR HEADPHONES

VERIFY CD
EQUIPMENT
SIZE AND POWER
REQUIREMENTS

SECURITY GATE

**AUDIO LISTENING KIOSK PLAN**

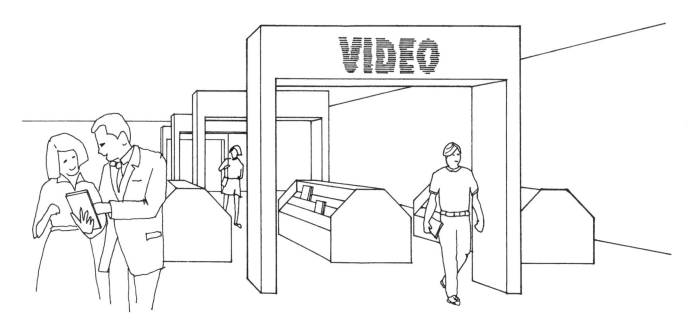

**SPACE DIVIDERS USED TO DELINEATE
CIRCULATION PLAN**

**SPACE DIVIDER USED TO DESIGNATE
DEPARTMENT**

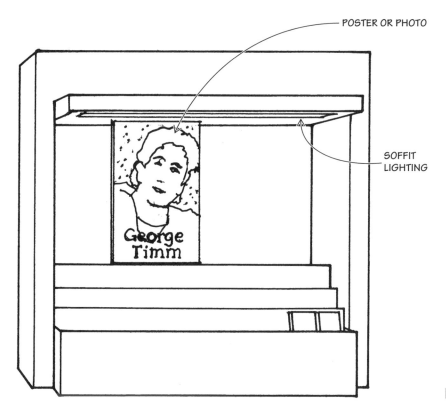

POSTER OR PHOTO

SOFFIT LIGHTING

George Timm

**BACK-TO-BACK HIGH DISPLAY**

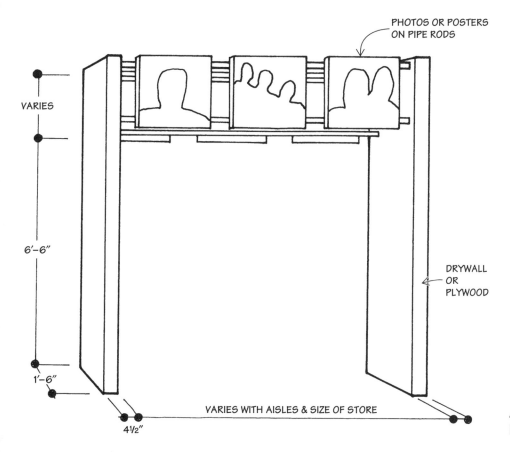

PHOTOS OR POSTERS ON PIPE RODS

VARIES

6'-6"

DRYWALL OR PLYWOOD

1'-6"

VARIES WITH AISLES & SIZE OF STORE

4½"

**ARCHED PORTAL TO DEPARTMENT**

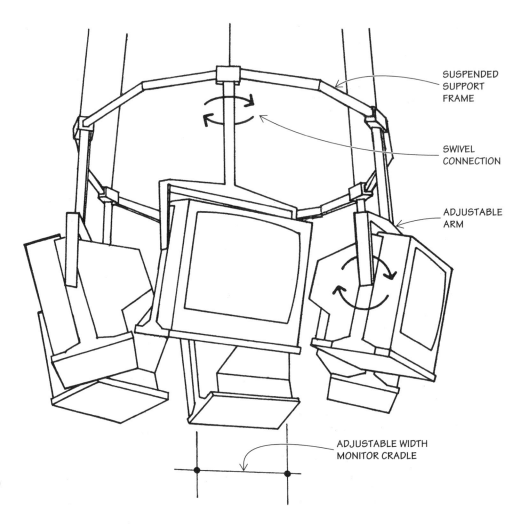

SUSPENDED
SUPPORT
FRAME

SWIVEL
CONNECTION

ADJUSTABLE
ARM

ADJUSTABLE WIDTH
MONITOR CRADLE

**CEILING-MOUNTED
VIDEO RING**

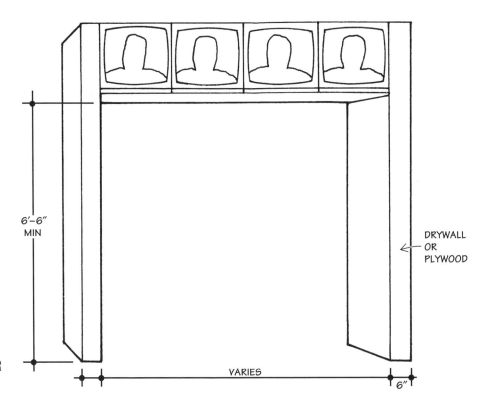

6'–6"
MIN

DRYWALL
OR
PLYWOOD

**VIDEO MONITOR
ARCHWAY**

VARIES

6"

- A video wall can become a dynamic focal point in any store.
- Screens can be programmed to achieve special effects such as repeat images and magnification of a single image.
- Video monitors are available in many sizes. Specific monitor screen and frame sizes, mounting, and power requirements should be verified with the manufacturer.
- Allow clearances around monitors for maintenance and proper ventilation per manufacturer's recommendations.

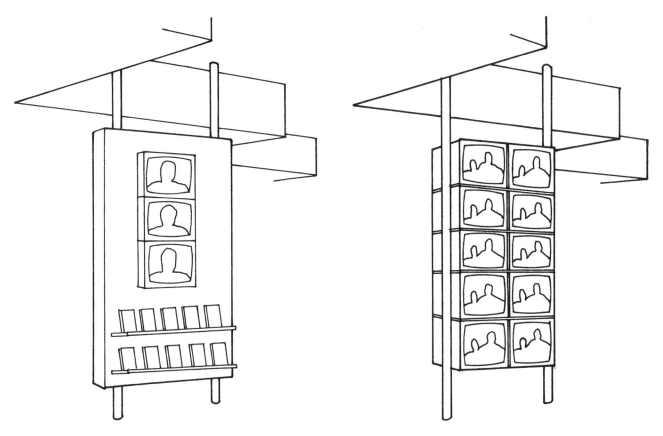

**VIDEO MONITOR AND MERCHANDISE
FEATURE**

**MULTIPLE VIDEO MONITOR TOWER**

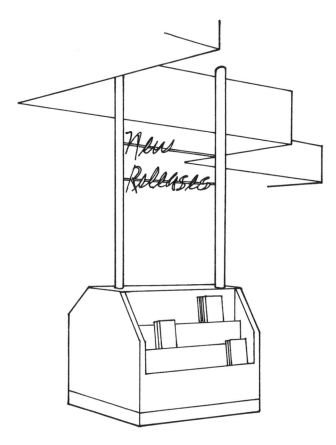

**MERCHANDISE DISPLAY ISLAND**

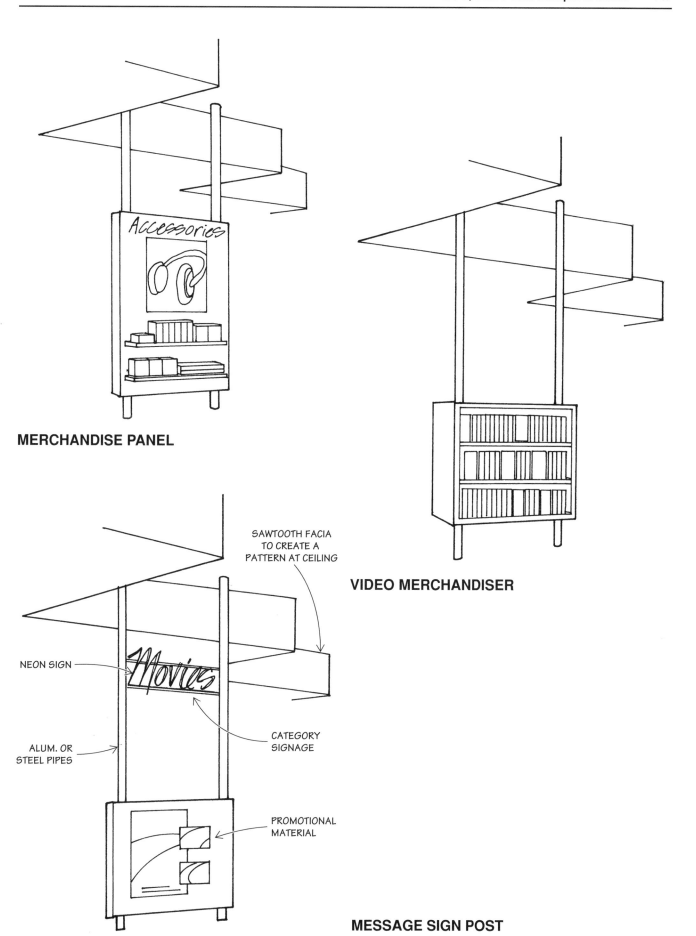

**MERCHANDISE PANEL**

**VIDEO MERCHANDISER**

SAWTOOTH FACIA
TO CREATE A
PATTERN AT CEILING

NEON SIGN

CATEGORY
SIGNAGE

ALUM. OR
STEEL PIPES

PROMOTIONAL
MATERIAL

**MESSAGE SIGN POST**

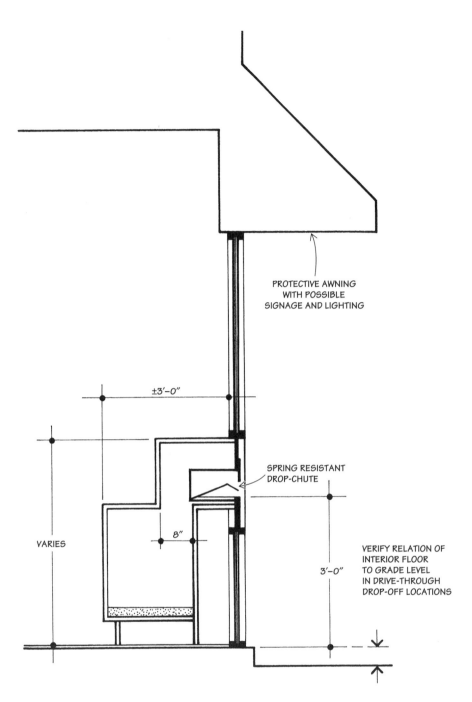

PROTECTIVE AWNING
WITH POSSIBLE
SIGNAGE AND LIGHTING

±3'-0"

SPRING RESISTANT
DROP-CHUTE

VARIES

8"

VERIFY RELATION OF
INTERIOR FLOOR
TO GRADE LEVEL
IN DRIVE-THROUGH
DROP-OFF LOCATIONS

3'-0"

**CROSS-SECTION OF VIDEO
DROP**

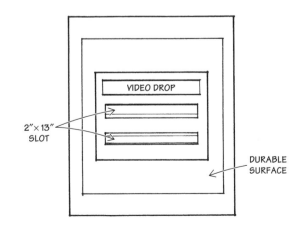

VIDEO DROP

2" × 13"
SLOT

DURABLE
SURFACE

**EXTERIOR VIDEO DROP**

# 12

# Science and Environmental Stores

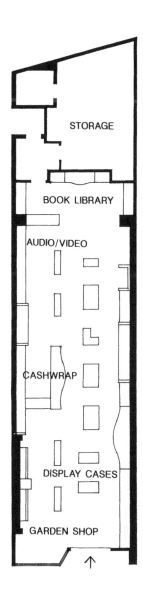

**SCIENCE AND
ENVIRONMENTAL
CHAIN STORE IN A
SHOPPING MALL**

Within the floor plan:
STORAGE
BOOK LIBRARY
AUDIO/VIDEO
CASHWRAP
DISPLAY CASES
GARDEN SHOP

## Tips and Guidelines

1. Broad assortment of merchandise is carried, in a wide variety of sizes and shapes.

   - Items range in size from pebbles to telescopes, and are priced from a few dollars to many thousands of dollars.

   - Provide security systems for open merchandise displays and for merchandise in enclosed cases.

2. Some areas of the store can be self-service; other merchandise is in showcases or behind counters and requires the assistance salesperson for examination.

3. Extend feeling of the natural environment; specify natural materials for casework and display units.

   - Add value to small impulse items by displaying them in specially designed casework.

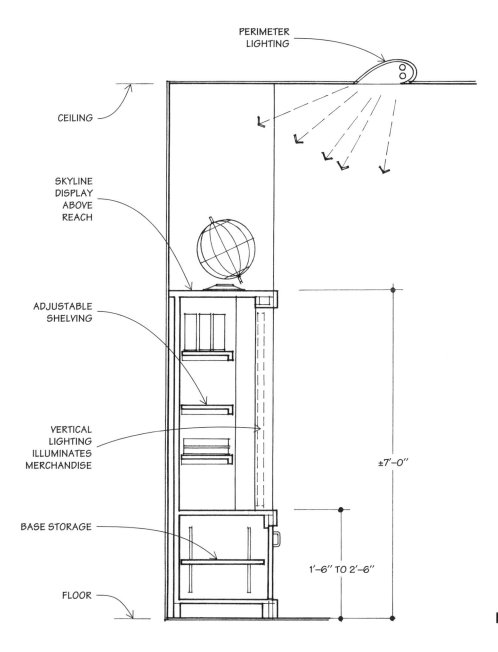

PERIMETER
LIGHTING

CEILING

SKYLINE
DISPLAY
ABOVE
REACH

ADJUSTABLE
SHELVING

VERTICAL
LIGHTING
ILLUMINATES
MERCHANDISE

BASE STORAGE

FLOOR

±7'–0"

1'–6" TO 2'–6"

**PERIMETER WALL UNIT**

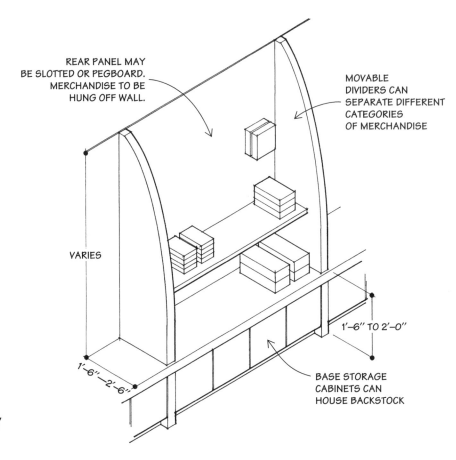

REAR PANEL MAY
BE SLOTTED OR PEGBOARD.
MERCHANDISE TO BE
HUNG OFF WALL.

MOVABLE
DIVIDERS CAN
SEPARATE DIFFERENT
CATEGORIES
OF MERCHANDISE

VARIES

1'-6" TO 2'-0"

1'-6" - 2'-6"

BASE STORAGE
CABINETS CAN
HOUSE BACKSTOCK

**MERCHANDISE DISPLAY
WALL**

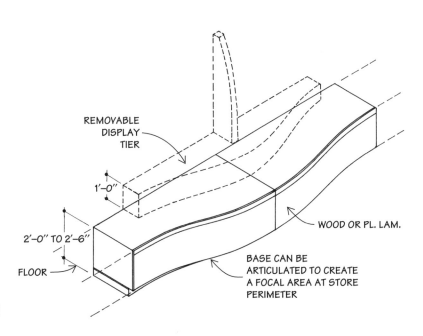

REMOVABLE
DISPLAY
TIER

1'-0"

2'-0" TO 2'-6"

WOOD OR PL. LAM.

BASE CAN BE
ARTICULATED TO CREATE
A FOCAL AREA AT STORE
PERIMETER

FLOOR

**PERIMETER DISPLAY BASE**

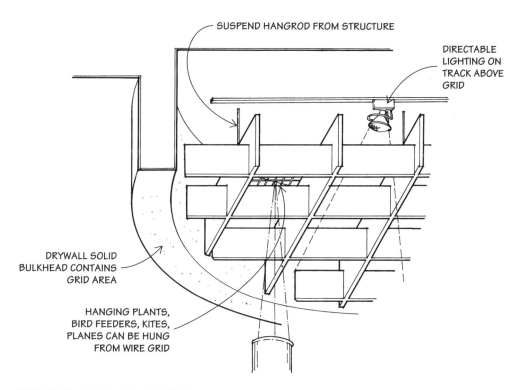

SUSPEND HANGROD FROM STRUCTURE

DIRECTABLE
LIGHTING ON
TRACK ABOVE
GRID

DRYWALL SOLID
BULKHEAD CONTAINS
GRID AREA

HANGING PLANTS,
BIRD FEEDERS, KITES,
PLANES CAN BE HUNG
FROM WIRE GRID

**CEILING TRELLIS DETAIL**

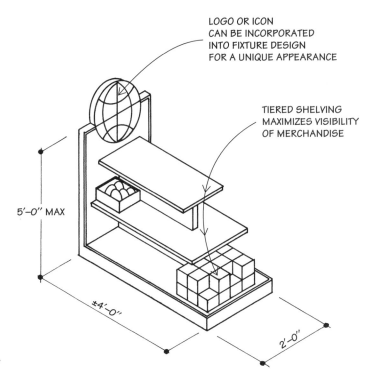

LOGO OR ICON
CAN BE INCORPORATED
INTO FIXTURE DESIGN
FOR A UNIQUE APPEARANCE

TIERED SHELVING
MAXIMIZES VISIBILITY
OF MERCHANDISE

5'-0" MAX

±4'-0"

2'-0"

**MERCHANDISE DISPLAY**

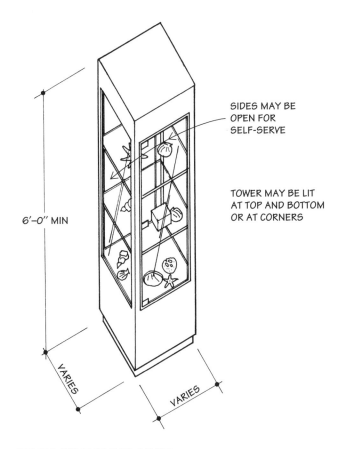

SIDES MAY BE
OPEN FOR
SELF-SERVE

TOWER MAY BE LIT
AT TOP AND BOTTOM
OR AT CORNERS

6'-0" MIN

VARIES

VARIES

**FREE-STANDING UNIT**

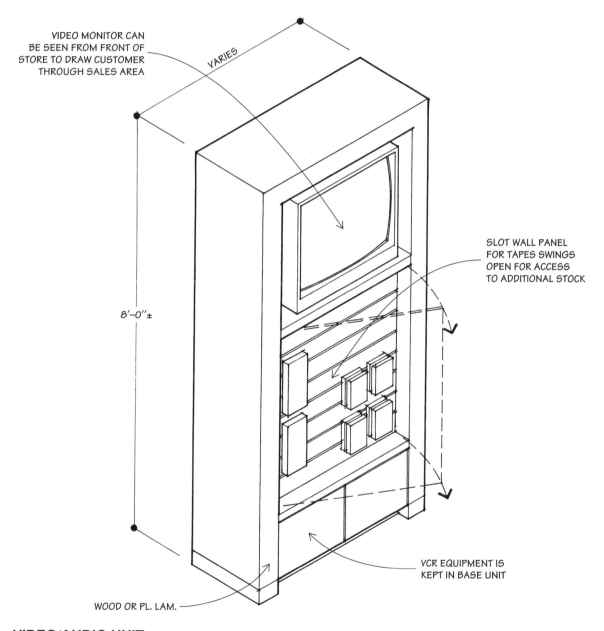

VIDEO MONITOR CAN
BE SEEN FROM FRONT OF
STORE TO DRAW CUSTOMER
THROUGH SALES AREA

VARIES

SLOT WALL PANEL
FOR TAPES SWINGS
OPEN FOR ACCESS
TO ADDITIONAL STOCK

8'–0''±

VCR EQUIPMENT IS
KEPT IN BASE UNIT

WOOD OR PL. LAM.

## VIDEO/AUDIO UNIT

## SKETCH OF TYPICAL SCIENCE AND ENVIRONMENTAL STORE

- Radial motif is reinforced in ceiling and floor articulation, angle of rear wall, fixture placement and spherical "globe" feature on wall.

- Tube and rib ceiling grid can support hanging signage and merchandise such as kites, mobiles, and planes or rockets.

- Wall recesses can be fitted with glass cases, shelves, or display panels for pegged merchandise.

- Mobile "sleigh" fixtures are flexible for many merchandising themes and work well as a repetitive design element.

- Books work well at the rear of a science or nature store as a destination department.

- Video monitors provide an ever-changing focus of activity.

# 13

# Baked Goods Shops

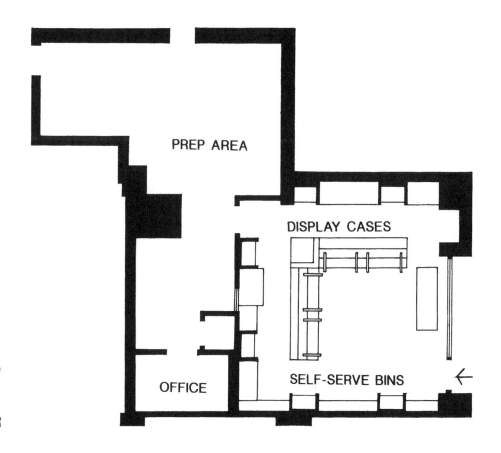

**STREETFRONT BAKED GOODS SHOP, SINGLE LEVEL, FOR AN INDEPENDENT OWNER**

PREP AREA

DISPLAY CASES

SELF-SERVE BINS

OFFICE

## Tips and Guidelines

1. There are two types of retail stores selling baked goods: those that have baking facilities on the premises, and those that sell baked goods that have been produced elsewhere.

   ▪ Most codes require both types of stores to provide facilities for employee hand washing on the premises.

2. Baked products should be protected by glass or plastic.

   ▪ The exception is prewrapped products.

3. Some baked products, such as decorated cakes, require a refrigerated display case.

   ▪ If baking is done on-site, additional refrigerated storage for raw materials is needed.

4. Coordinate installation of utilities and ventilation with the HVAC engineer.

   ▪ Design attractive housing for baking equipment that will be within customers' sight.

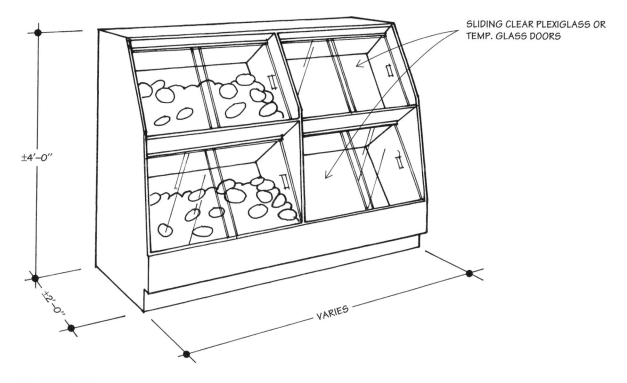

SLIDING CLEAR PLEXIGLASS OR
TEMP. GLASS DOORS

±4'–0"

±2'–0"

VARIES

**CLOSED BIN DISPLAY**

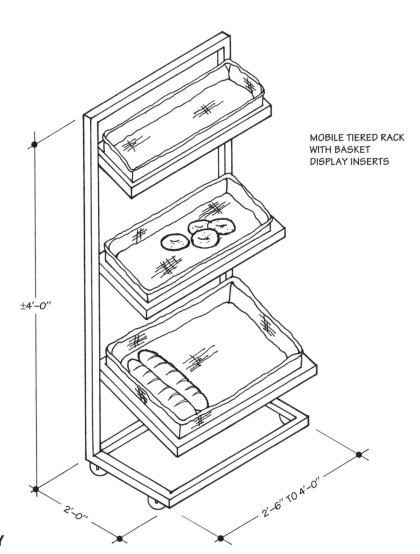

MOBILE TIERED RACK
WITH BASKET
DISPLAY INSERTS

±4'-0"

2'-0"

2'-6" TO 4'-0"

**MOVABLE CART DISPLAY**

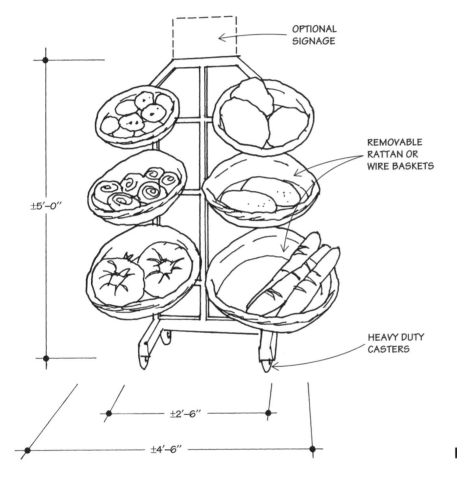

OPTIONAL
SIGNAGE

REMOVABLE
RATTAN OR
WIRE BASKETS

HEAVY DUTY
CASTERS

±5'-0"

±2'-6"

±4'-6"

**BASKET DISPLAY**

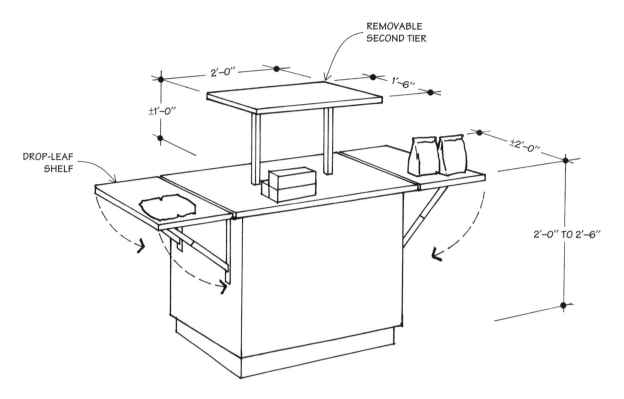

REMOVABLE
SECOND TIER

2'-0''

1'-6''

±1'-0''

DROP-LEAF
SHELF

±2'-0''

2'-0'' TO 2'-6''

**TABLETOP DISPLAY**

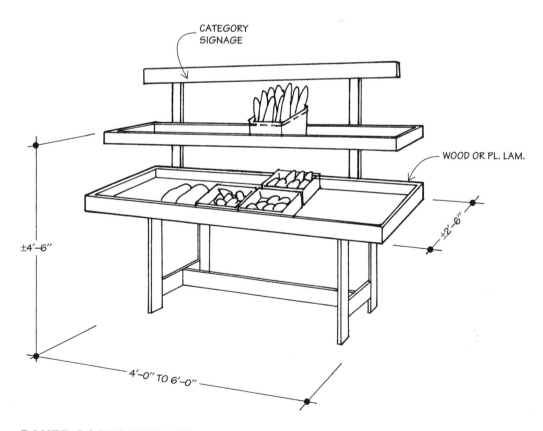

CATEGORY
SIGNAGE

WOOD OR PL. LAM.

±4'-6''

±2'-6''

4'-0'' TO 6'-0''

**BAKED GOODS DISPLAY**

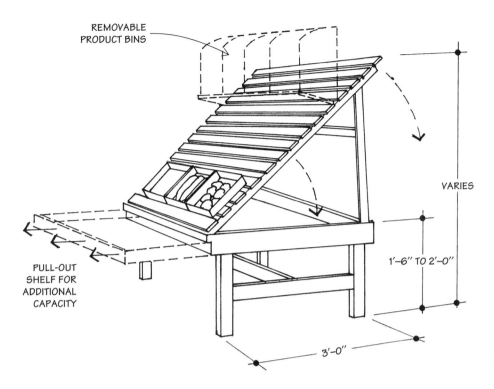

REMOVABLE PRODUCT BINS

VARIES

1'-6" TO 2'-0"

PULL-OUT SHELF FOR ADDITIONAL CAPACITY

3'-0"

**ADJUSTABLE SLATTED WOOD DISPLAY**

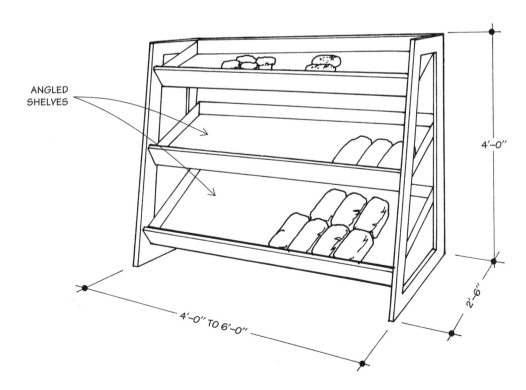

ANGLED SHELVES

4'-0"

2'-6"

4'-0" TO 6'-0"

**SLOPED TIERED SHELF DISPLAY**

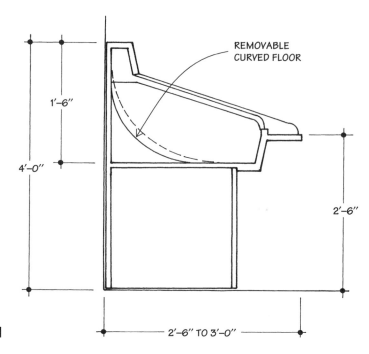

1'-6''

4'-0''

REMOVABLE
CURVED FLOOR

2'-6''

2'-6'' TO 3'-0''

**SECTION THROUGH BAGEL BIN**

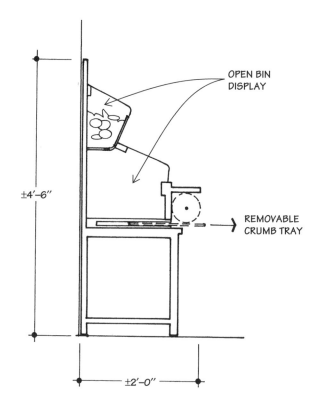

±4'-6''

OPEN BIN
DISPLAY

REMOVABLE
CRUMB TRAY

±2'-0''

**SECTION THROUGH OPEN BINS**

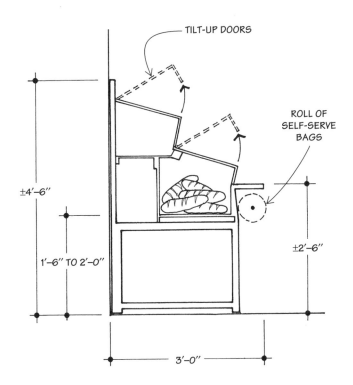

TILT-UP DOORS

ROLL OF
SELF-SERVE
BAGS

±4'–6"

1'–6" TO 2'–0"

±2'–6"

3'–0"

**SECTION THROUGH CLOSED BIN**

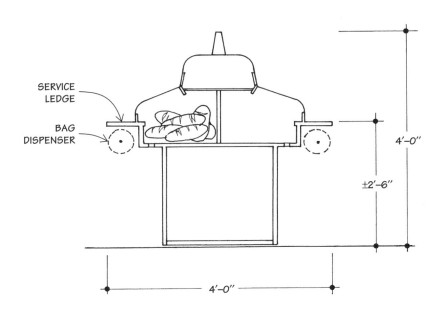

SERVICE
LEDGE

BAG
DISPENSER

4'–0"

±2'–6"

4'–0"

**SECTION THROUGH TIERED
BAKED GOODS ISLAND**

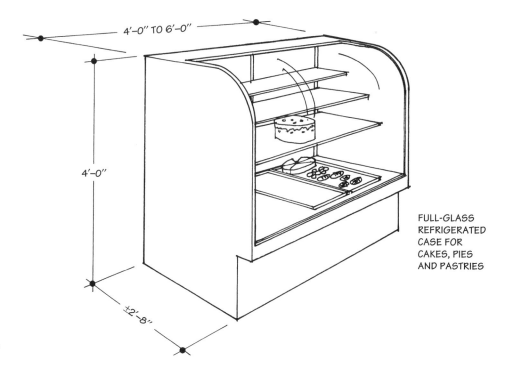

4'–0" TO 6'–0"

4'–0"

±2'–8"

FULL-GLASS
REFRIGERATED
CASE FOR
CAKES, PIES
AND PASTRIES

**CAKE DISPLAY**

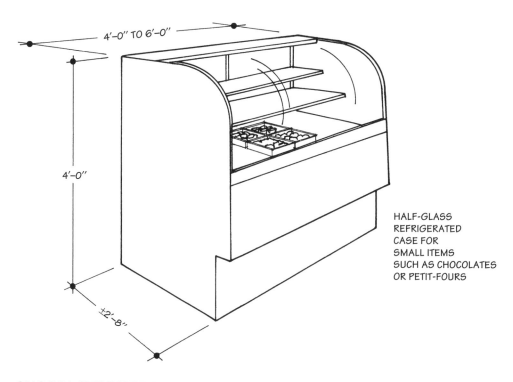

4'–0" TO 6'–0"

4'–0"

±2'–8"

HALF-GLASS
REFRIGERATED
CASE FOR
SMALL ITEMS
SUCH AS CHOCOLATES
OR PETIT-FOURS

**CHOCOLATE DISPLAY**

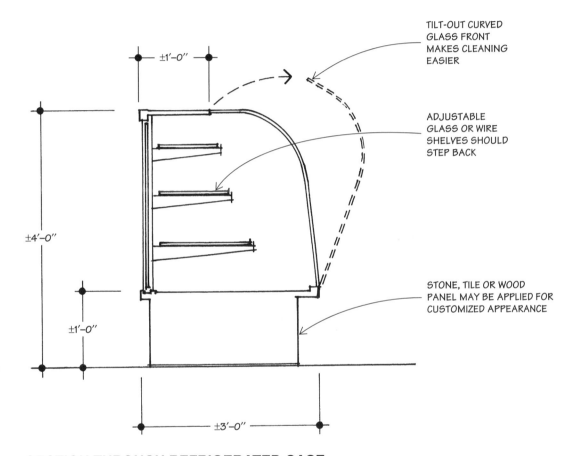

TILT-OUT CURVED
GLASS FRONT
MAKES CLEANING
EASIER

ADJUSTABLE
GLASS OR WIRE
SHELVES SHOULD
STEP BACK

STONE, TILE OR WOOD
PANEL MAY BE APPLIED FOR
CUSTOMIZED APPEARANCE

±1'-0"

±4'-0"

±1'-0"

±3'-0"

## SECTION THROUGH REFRIGERATED CASE

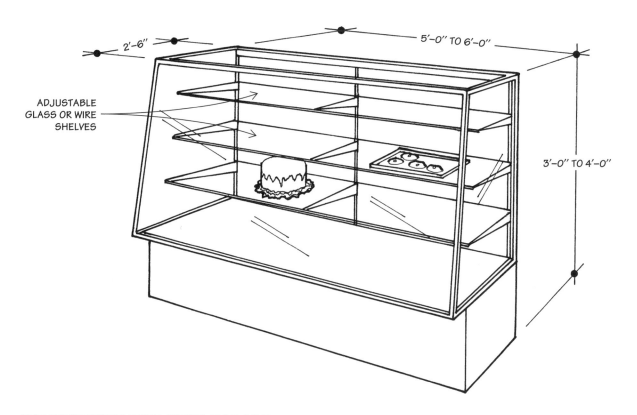

2'-6"

5'-0" TO 6'-0"

ADJUSTABLE
GLASS OR WIRE
SHELVES

3'-0" TO 4'-0"

**NONREFRIGERATED DISPLAY CASE**

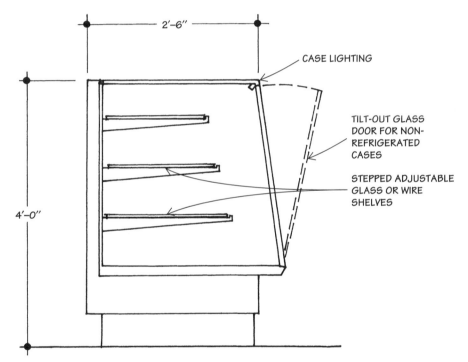

2'-6"

4'-0"

CASE LIGHTING

TILT-OUT GLASS
DOOR FOR NON-
REFRIGERATED
CASES

STEPPED ADJUSTABLE
GLASS OR WIRE
SHELVES

**SECTION THROUGH
NONREFRIGERATED
DISPLAY CASE**

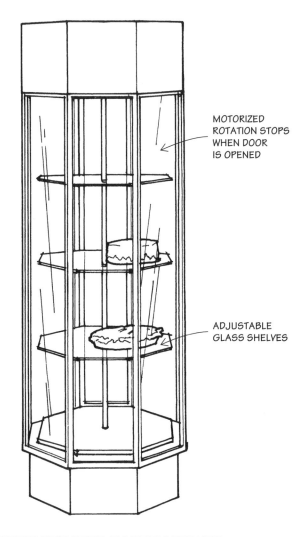

MOTORIZED
ROTATION STOPS
WHEN DOOR
IS OPENED

ADJUSTABLE
GLASS SHELVES

**REFRIGERATED PASTRY TOWER**

# 14

# Card and Stationery Shops

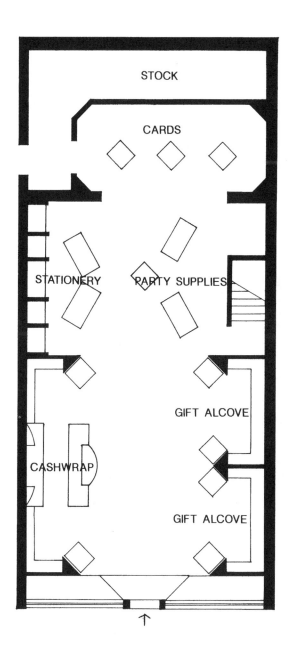

STOCK

CARDS

STATIONERY

PARTY SUPPLIES

GIFT ALCOVE

CASHWRAP

GIFT ALCOVE

**INDEPENDENTLY
OWNED CARD SHOP IN
A STRIP MALL**

## Tips and Guidelines

1. This category includes (a) stores that concentrate on greeting cards, paper goods, and gifts, and (b) stores that handle basic office supplies.

   - Layout and fixtures for stores in "a" group are sometimes supplied by major industry vendors.

   - Stores in "b" group may also display a limited line of office equipment, such as files, desks, and chairs.

2. Consultation area, horizontal viewing surface, and storage for sample books will facilitate customer selection of custom printing for personal and business use.

3. Store designer can add to customer's perception of value of inexpensive items with imaginative display fixtures and interesting use of materials.

4. Products such as higher-priced writing instruments and gift items are displayed in showcases.

   - Security systems should be installed for merchandise protection and theft control.

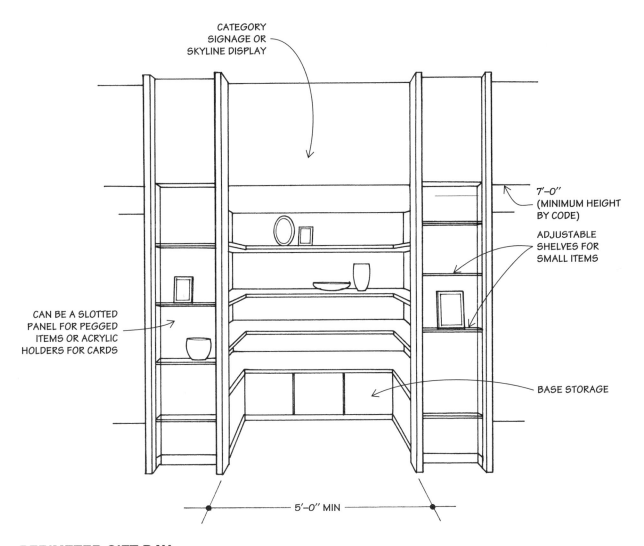

CATEGORY
SIGNAGE OR
SKYLINE DISPLAY

7'-0''
(MINIMUM HEIGHT
BY CODE)

ADJUSTABLE
SHELVES FOR
SMALL ITEMS

CAN BE A SLOTTED
PANEL FOR PEGGED
ITEMS OR ACRYLIC
HOLDERS FOR CARDS

BASE STORAGE

5'-0'' MIN

**PERIMETER GIFT BAY**

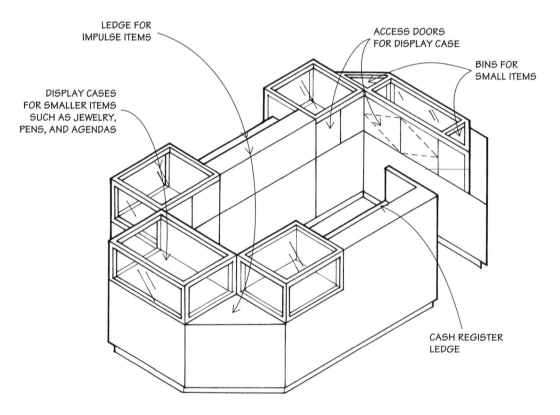

LEDGE FOR
IMPULSE ITEMS

ACCESS DOORS
FOR DISPLAY CASE

BINS FOR
SMALL ITEMS

DISPLAY CASES
FOR SMALLER ITEMS
SUCH AS JEWELRY,
PENS, AND AGENDAS

CASH REGISTER
LEDGE

**ISLAND CASHWRAP**

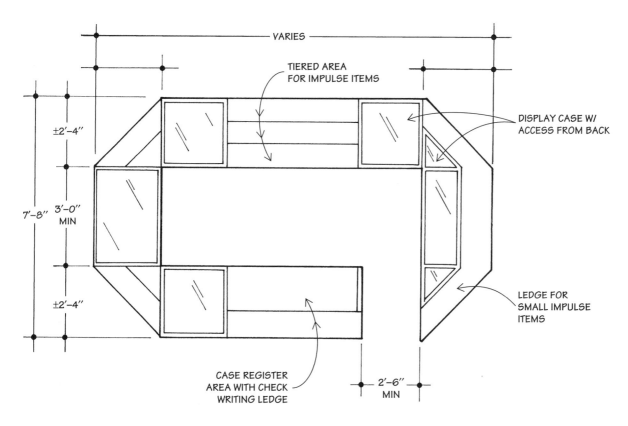

NOTE: VERIFY A.D.A. REQUIREMENTS
FOR CASH WRAP ACCESSIBILITY

**PLAN OF FLOATING CASHWRAP**

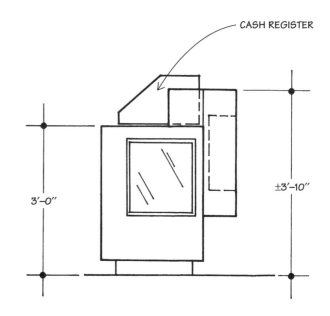

CASH REGISTER

3'-0"

±3'-10"

**CASHWRAP SIDE ELEVATION**

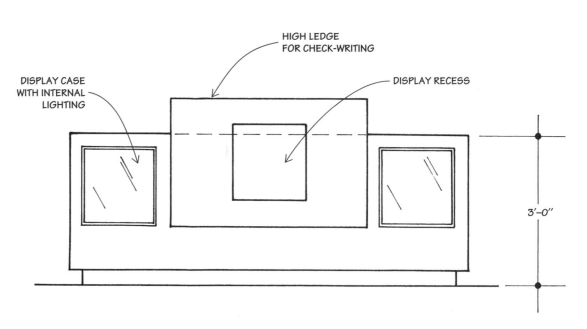

HIGH LEDGE
FOR CHECK-WRITING

DISPLAY CASE
WITH INTERNAL
LIGHTING

DISPLAY RECESS

3'-0"

**CASHWRAP FRONT ELEVATION**

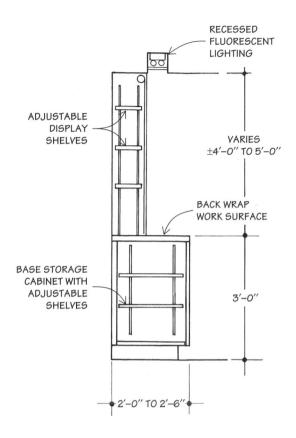

RECESSED
FLUORESCENT
LIGHTING

ADJUSTABLE
DISPLAY
SHELVES

VARIES
±4'-0" TO 5'-0"

BACK WRAP
WORK SURFACE

BASE STORAGE
CABINET WITH
ADJUSTABLE
SHELVES

3'-0"

2'-0" TO 2'-6"

## SECTION AT BACKWRAP

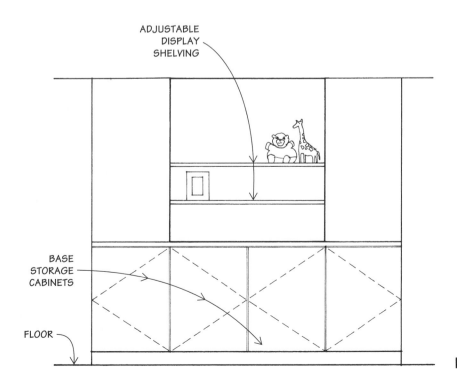

ADJUSTABLE
DISPLAY
SHELVING

BASE
STORAGE
CABINETS

FLOOR

## BACKWRAP ELEVATION

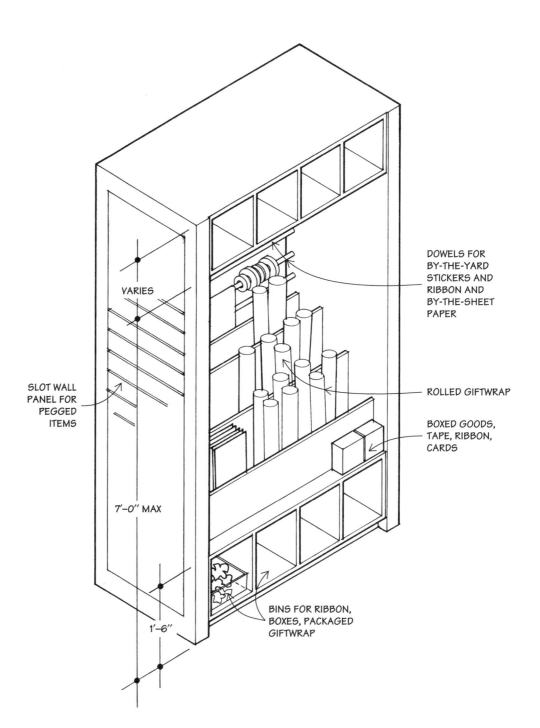

VARIES

DOWELS FOR
BY-THE-YARD
STICKERS AND
RIBBON AND
BY-THE-SHEET
PAPER

SLOT WALL
PANEL FOR
PEGGED
ITEMS

ROLLED GIFTWRAP

BOXED GOODS,
TAPE, RIBBON,
CARDS

7'-0" MAX

1'-6"

BINS FOR RIBBON,
BOXES, PACKAGED
GIFTWRAP

**PAPER GOODS DISPLAY UNIT**

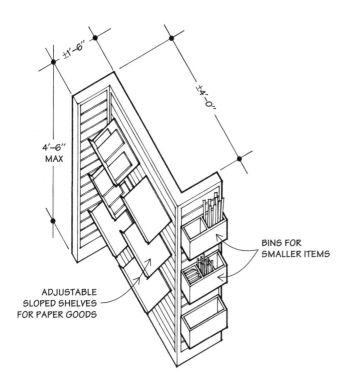

±1'-6"

±4'-0"

4'-6"
MAX

BINS FOR
SMALLER ITEMS

ADJUSTABLE
SLOPED SHELVES
FOR PAPER GOODS

**Z-SHAPE SLATWALL UNIT**

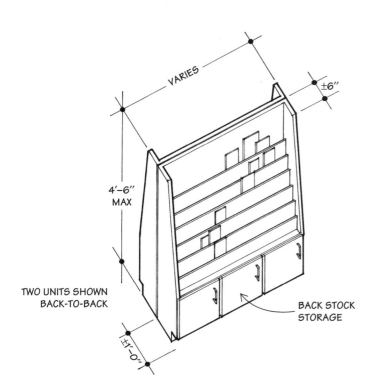

VARIES

±6"

4'-6"
MAX

TWO UNITS SHOWN
BACK-TO-BACK

BACK STOCK
STORAGE

±1'-0"

**GREETING CARD RACKS**

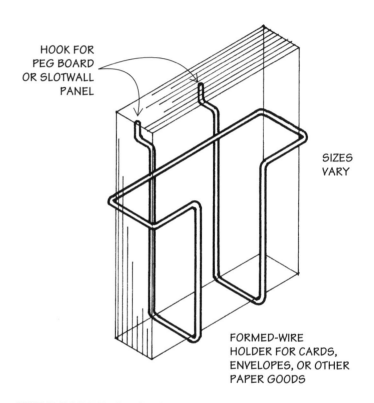

HOOK FOR
PEG BOARD
OR SLOTWALL
PANEL

SIZES
VARY

FORMED-WIRE
HOLDER FOR CARDS,
ENVELOPES, OR OTHER
PAPER GOODS

**WIRE PAPER-GOODS HOLDER**

# 15

# Jewelry Stores

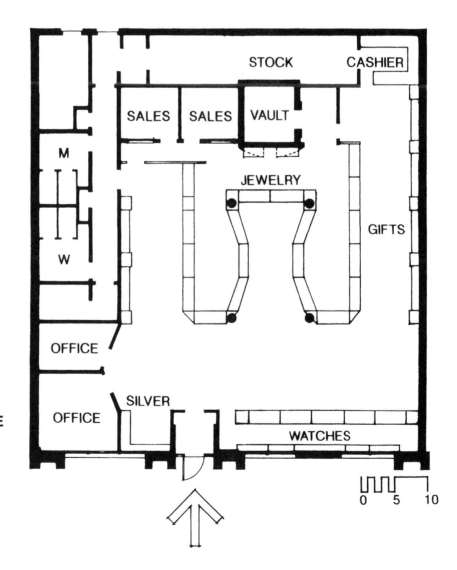

INDEPENDENTLY OWNED JEWELRY STORE IN A SUBURBAN AREA. THE STORE, WHICH HAS BEEN REMODELED, IS FREE-STANDING AS PART OF A SMALL STRIP CENTER, AND HAS HIGHWAY FRONTAGE

## Tips and Guidelines

1. Retail operations carrying high-value merchandise require security systems for the store and to protect the displays and back-up inventory.

   - Enclosed showcases should resist "smash-and-grab" attacks.

2. Most jewelry stores are service-oriented rather than self-service operations. Consider:

   - The perceptions of the customer purchasing the high-end product.
   - The relationship of the customer and the salesperson.
   - The customer's comfort.

3. Lighting plays a dominant role in the nonverbal communication of the sales appeal of the jewelry.

   - Use spotlighting to highlight the merchandise.
   - Illuminate the interior of the display case.
   - Illuminate the display case or other surface where the customer will examine the merchandise.
   - Ambient lighting should be selected to complement product lighting.

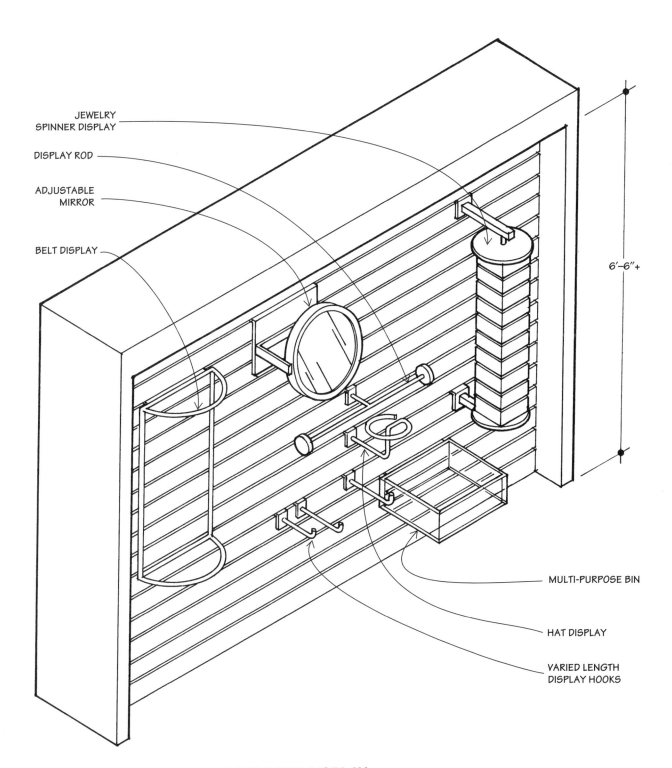

JEWELRY
SPINNER DISPLAY

DISPLAY ROD

ADJUSTABLE
MIRROR

BELT DISPLAY

6'-6"+

MULTI-PURPOSE BIN

HAT DISPLAY

VARIED LENGTH
DISPLAY HOOKS

**COSTUME JEWELRY AND ACCESSORY DISPLAY**

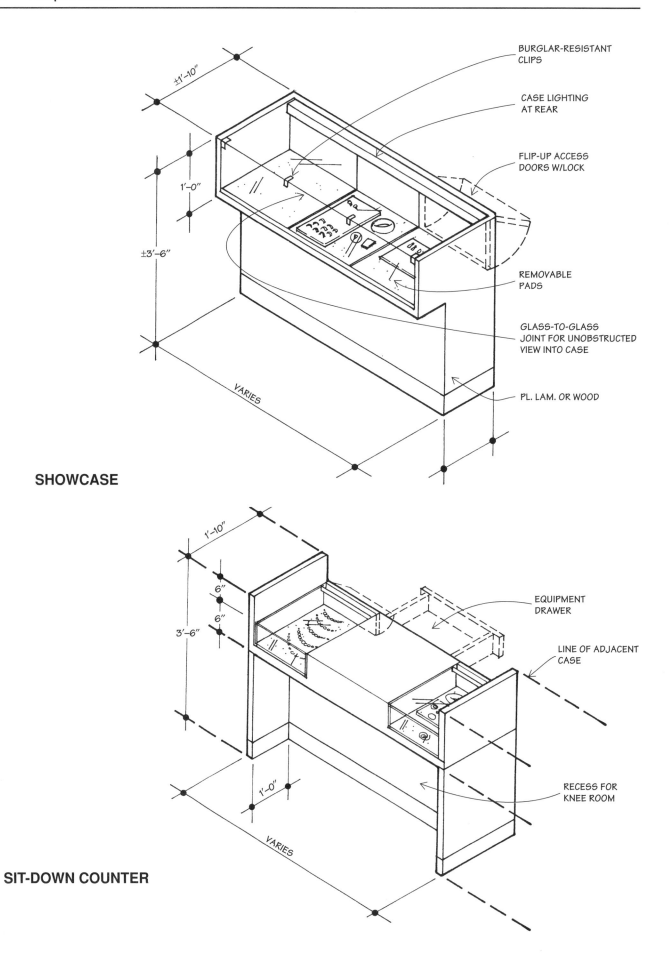

±1'-10"

BURGLAR-RESISTANT
CLIPS

CASE LIGHTING
AT REAR

1'-0"

FLIP-UP ACCESS
DOORS W/LOCK

±3'-6"

REMOVABLE
PADS

GLASS-TO-GLASS
JOINT FOR UNOBSTRUCTED
VIEW INTO CASE

VARIES

PL. LAM. OR WOOD

**SHOWCASE**

1'-10"

6"

EQUIPMENT
DRAWER

6"

3'-6"

LINE OF ADJACENT
CASE

1'-0"

RECESS FOR
KNEE ROOM

VARIES

**SIT-DOWN COUNTER**

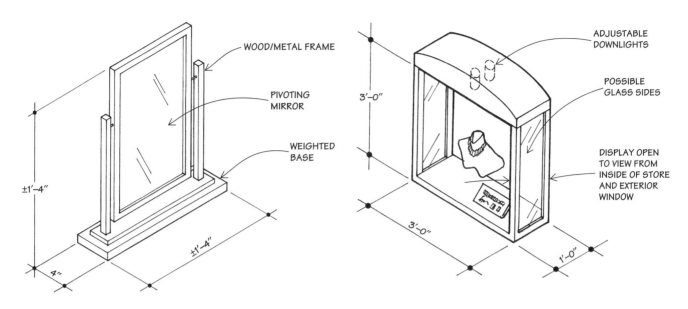

WOOD/METAL FRAME

PIVOTING MIRROR

WEIGHTED BASE

±1'-4"

±1'-4"

4"

**COUNTERTOP MIRROR**

ADJUSTABLE DOWNLIGHTS

POSSIBLE GLASS SIDES

DISPLAY OPEN TO VIEW FROM INSIDE OF STORE AND EXTERIOR WINDOW

3'-0"

3'-0"

1'-0"

**WINDOW SHADOWBOX**

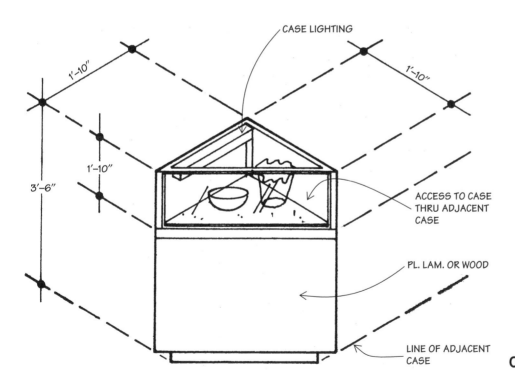

CASE LIGHTING

1'-10"

1'-10"

1'-10"

3'-6"

ACCESS TO CASE THRU ADJACENT CASE

PL. LAM. OR WOOD

LINE OF ADJACENT CASE

**CORNER SHOWCASE**

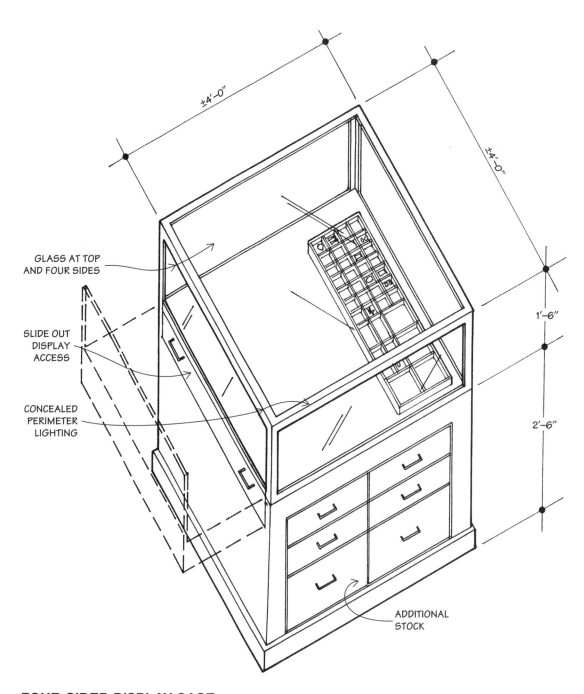

±4'-0"

±4'-0"

1'-6"

2'-6"

GLASS AT TOP
AND FOUR SIDES

SLIDE OUT
DISPLAY
ACCESS

CONCEALED
PERIMETER
LIGHTING

ADDITIONAL
STOCK

**FOUR-SIDED DISPLAY CASE**

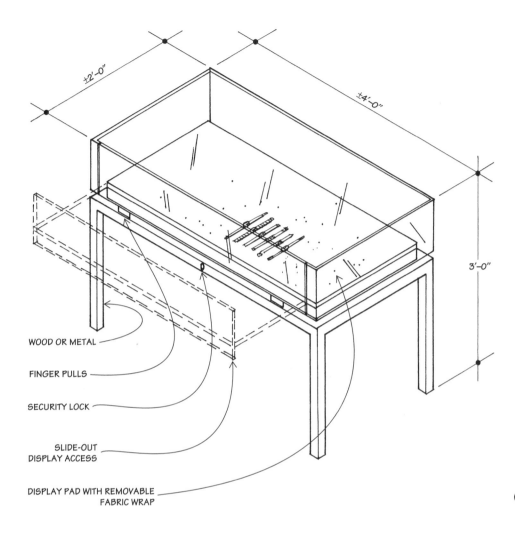

±2'-0"

±4'-0"

3'-0"

WOOD OR METAL

FINGER PULLS

SECURITY LOCK

SLIDE-OUT
DISPLAY ACCESS

DISPLAY PAD WITH REMOVABLE
FABRIC WRAP

**GLASS SHOWCASE**

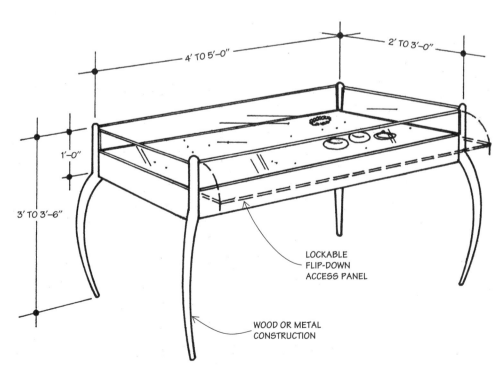

4' TO 5'-0"

2' TO 3'-0"

1'-0"

3' TO 3'-6"

LOCKABLE
FLIP-DOWN
ACCESS PANEL

WOOD OR METAL
CONSTRUCTION

**FREE-STANDING SHOWCASE**

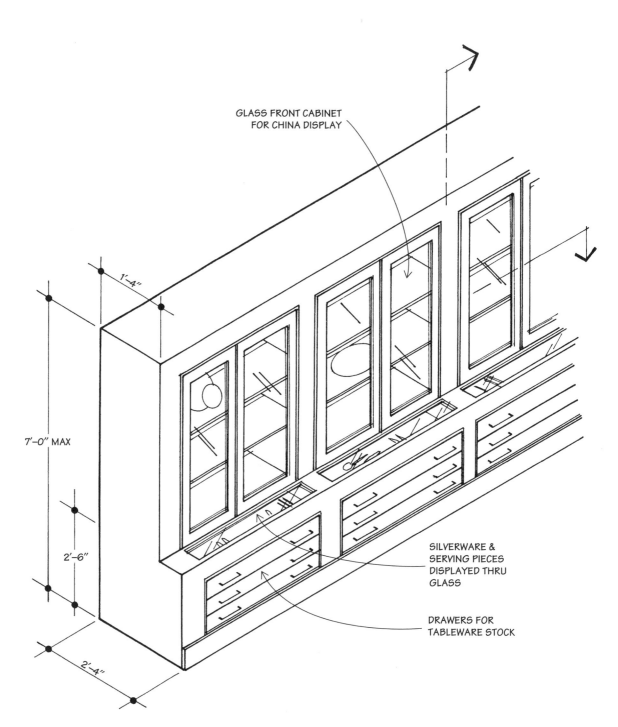

GLASS FRONT CABINET
FOR CHINA DISPLAY

1'-4"

7'-0" MAX

2'-6"

2'-4"

SILVERWARE &
SERVING PIECES
DISPLAYED THRU
GLASS

DRAWERS FOR
TABLEWARE STOCK

**TABLETOP DISPLAY**

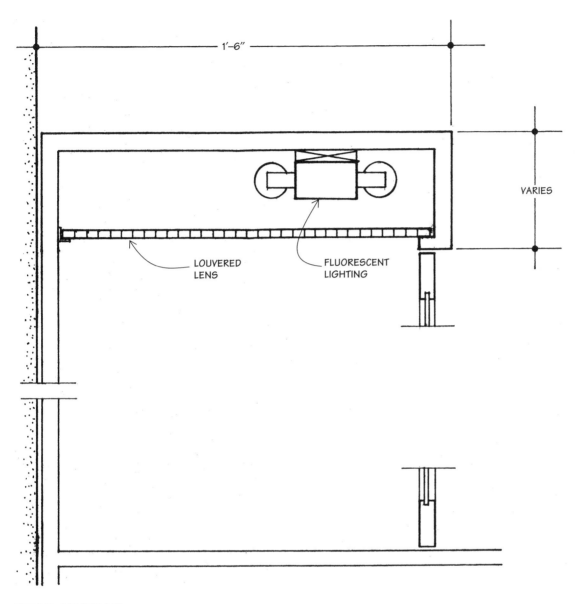

1'-6"

VARIES

LOUVERED
LENS

FLUORESCENT
LIGHTING

**HEAD SECTION**

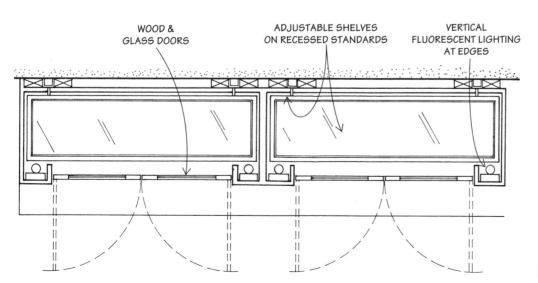

WOOD &
GLASS DOORS

ADJUSTABLE SHELVES
ON RECESSED STANDARDS

VERTICAL
FLUORESCENT LIGHTING
AT EDGES

**PLAN SECTION**

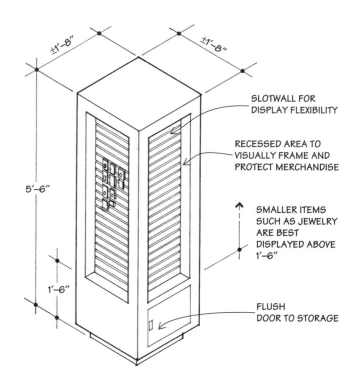

±1'-8"   ±1'-8"

SLOTWALL FOR
DISPLAY FLEXIBILITY

RECESSED AREA TO
VISUALLY FRAME AND
PROTECT MERCHANDISE

5'-6"

SMALLER ITEMS
SUCH AS JEWELRY
ARE BEST
DISPLAYED ABOVE
1'-6"

1'-6"

FLUSH
DOOR TO STORAGE

## EARRING AND JEWELRY ON-CARD DISPLAY

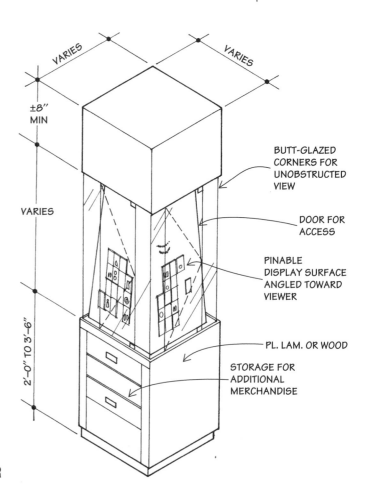

VARIES     VARIES

±8"
MIN

BUTT-GLAZED
CORNERS FOR
UNOBSTRUCTED
VIEW

DOOR FOR
ACCESS

VARIES

PINABLE
DISPLAY SURFACE
ANGLED TOWARD
VIEWER

PL. LAM. OR WOOD

2'-0" TO 3'-6"

STORAGE FOR
ADDITIONAL
MERCHANDISE

## JEWELRY TOWER

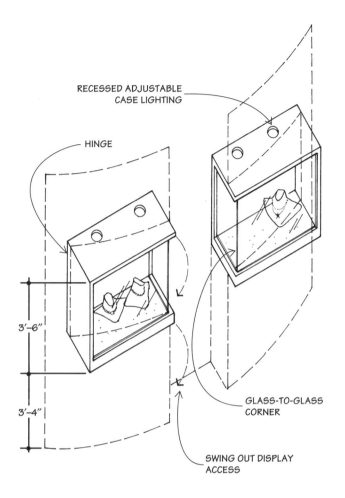

RECESSED ADJUSTABLE
CASE LIGHTING

HINGE

3'-6"

3'-4"

GLASS-TO-GLASS
CORNER

SWING OUT DISPLAY
ACCESS

**WALL DISPLAY CASE**

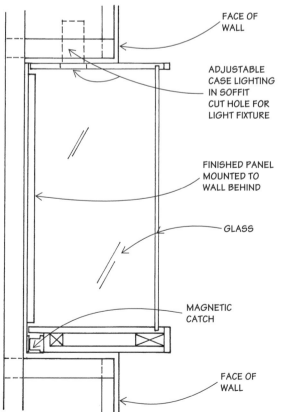

FACE OF
WALL

ADJUSTABLE
CASE LIGHTING
IN SOFFIT
CUT HOLE FOR
LIGHT FIXTURE

FINISHED PANEL
MOUNTED TO
WALL BEHIND

GLASS

MAGNETIC
CATCH

FACE OF
WALL

**VERTICAL CROSS-SECTION, WALL DISPLAY
CASE**

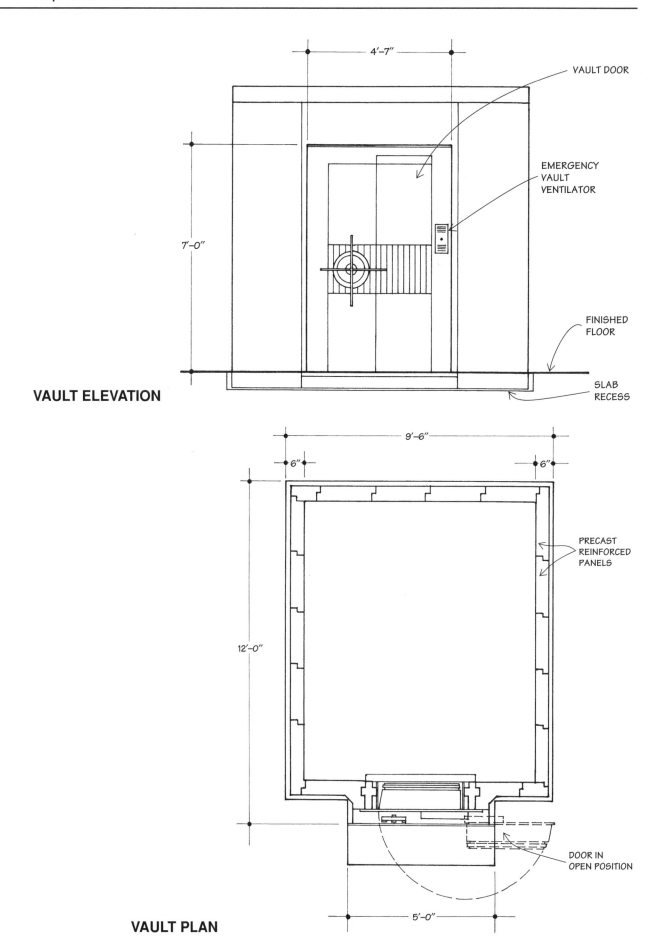

**VAULT ELEVATION**

**VAULT PLAN**

# 16

# Flower Shops

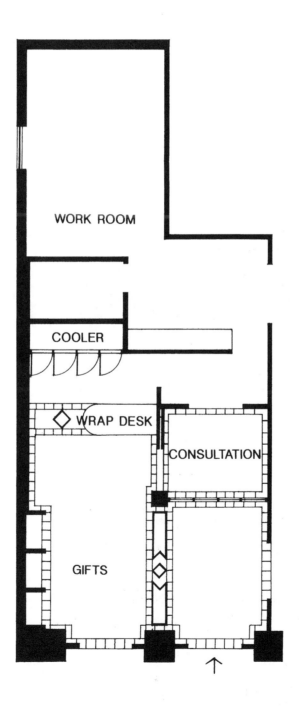

**WORK ROOM**

**COOLER**

◇ WRAP DESK

CONSULTATION

GIFTS

**FLOWER SHOP
LOCATED IN THE
LOBBY OF A
DOWNTOWN HOTEL**

## Tips and Guidelines

1. In addition to fresh-cut flowers, florists may also carry plants, artificial flowers, vases and jardinieres, and bulbs and seeds.

   - Some florists have also begun to handle small antiques items.

2. Refrigerators with sliding glass doors contain cut flower selection.

   - Place toward the rear of the store to pull traffic from front to back.

3. Merchandise presentation techniques include adjustable shelving, tabletops, and movable multilevel display stands.

4. Provide work areas for creating flower arrangements and wrapping customer purchases in the back of the shop, near the checkout or cashwrap station.

   - Provide for back area water supply, drains, nonpermeable work surfaces, and a holding area for floral arrangements awaiting delivery or pickup.

5. For florists whose business involves providing flowers for events, design a conference space appropriate for client meetings and furnished with tables, chairs, etc.

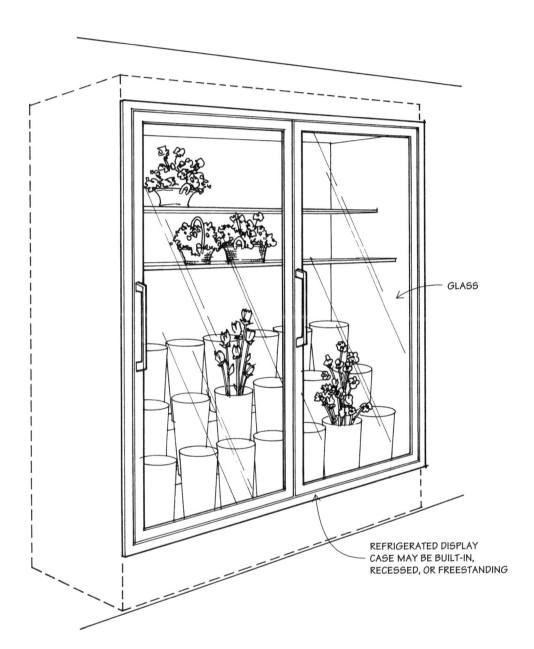

GLASS

REFRIGERATED DISPLAY
CASE MAY BE BUILT-IN,
RECESSED, OR FREESTANDING

**DISPLAY CASE**

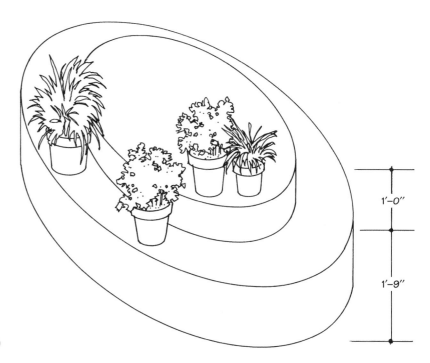

**OVAL DISPLAY ISLAND**

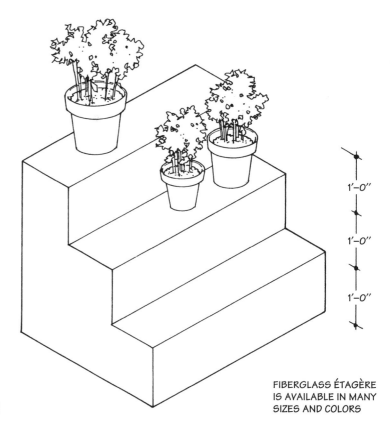

**TIERED ÉTAGÈRE**

FIBERGLASS ÉTAGÈRE
IS AVAILABLE IN MANY
SIZES AND COLORS

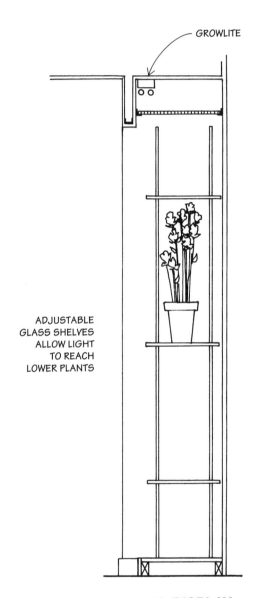

GROWLITE

ADJUSTABLE
GLASS SHELVES
ALLOW LIGHT
TO REACH
LOWER PLANTS

**SECTION THROUGH WALL DISPLAY**

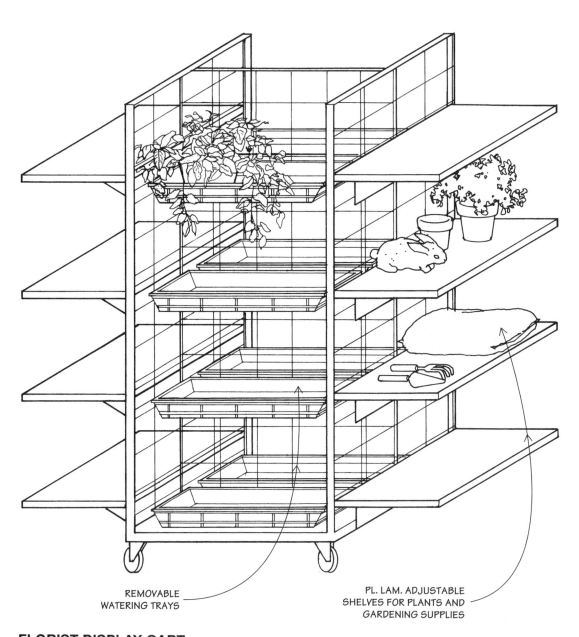

REMOVABLE
WATERING TRAYS

PL. LAM. ADJUSTABLE
SHELVES FOR PLANTS AND
GARDENING SUPPLIES

**FLORIST DISPLAY CART**

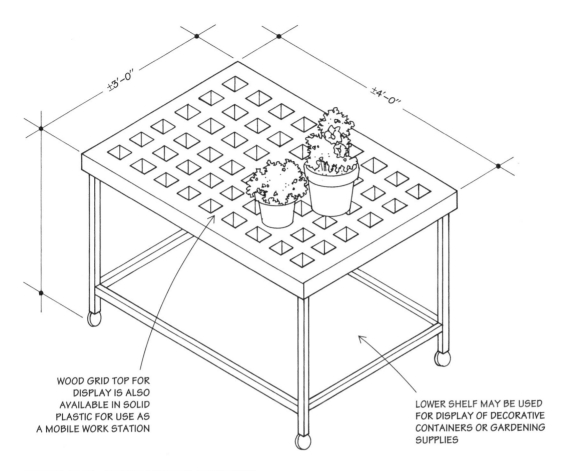

WOOD GRID TOP FOR
DISPLAY IS ALSO
AVAILABLE IN SOLID
PLASTIC FOR USE AS
A MOBILE WORK STATION

LOWER SHELF MAY BE USED
FOR DISPLAY OF DECORATIVE
CONTAINERS OR GARDENING
SUPPLIES

## MOBILE FLORIST WORK STATION

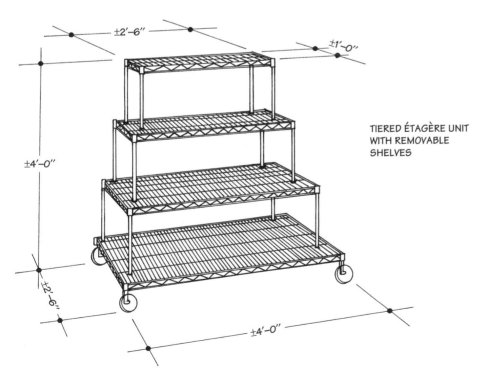

TIERED ÉTAGÈRE UNIT
WITH REMOVABLE
SHELVES

## TIERED ÉTAGÈRE UNIT
## WITH REMOVABLE
## SHELVES

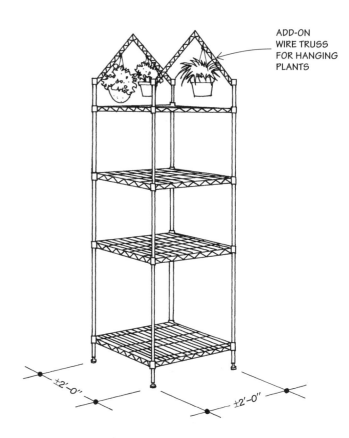

ADD-ON
WIRE TRUSS
FOR HANGING
PLANTS

±2'-0"

±2'-0"

**WIRE FLORIST DISPLAY UNIT**

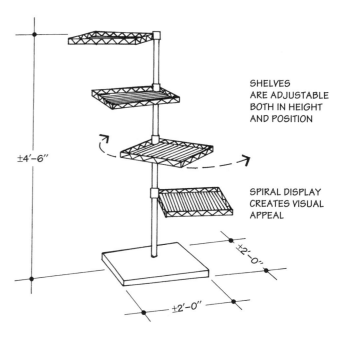

SHELVES
ARE ADJUSTABLE
BOTH IN HEIGHT
AND POSITION

SPIRAL DISPLAY
CREATES VISUAL
APPEAL

±4'-6"

±2'-0"

±2'-0"

**SWIVEL DISPLAY UNIT**

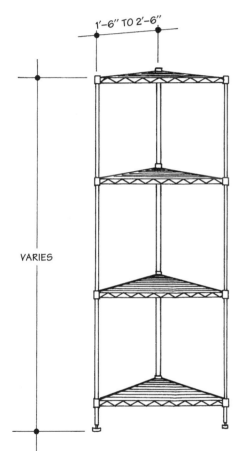

1'-6" TO 2'-6"

VARIES

TRIANGULAR DISPLAY
UNIT CAN BE USED
IN CORNERS OR AT
ENDS OF RECTANGULAR
ROWS OF SHELVING

**TRIANGULAR DISPLAY UNIT**

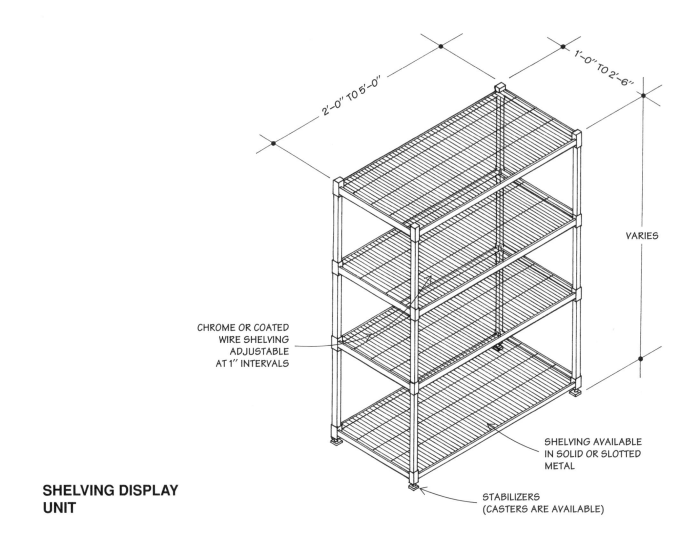

2'-0" TO 5'-0"

1'-0" TO 2'-6"

VARIES

CHROME OR COATED
WIRE SHELVING
ADJUSTABLE
AT 1" INTERVALS

SHELVING AVAILABLE
IN SOLID OR SLOTTED
METAL

STABILIZERS
(CASTERS ARE AVAILABLE)

**SHELVING DISPLAY
UNIT**

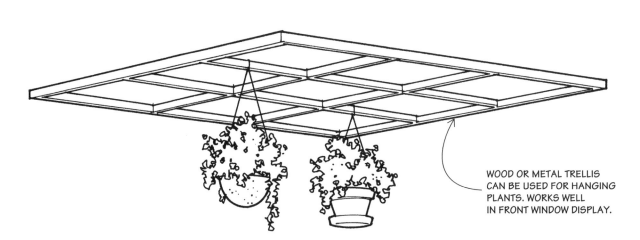

WOOD OR METAL TRELLIS
CAN BE USED FOR HANGING
PLANTS. WORKS WELL
IN FRONT WINDOW DISPLAY.

**HANGING BASKET DISPLAY**

# 17

# Optical Shops

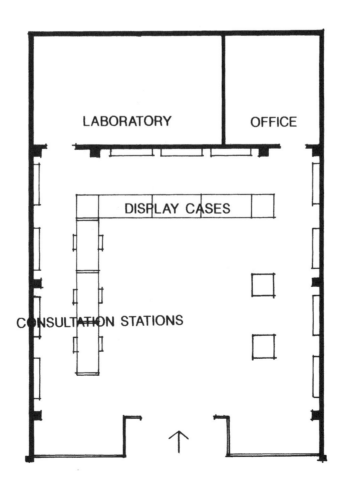

**OPTICAL SHOP
LOCATED IN A
SHOPPING CENTER**

LABORATORY

OFFICE

DISPLAY CASES

CONSULTATION STATIONS

## Tips and Guidelines

1. Eyeglasses have become a fashion business, and optical shops have both a style and function orientation.

   - An eyeglass store can be part of a chain, a franchise, or privately owned and operated.

2. Some optical shops offer eye examinations performed by a doctor on-site.

   - Separate private space with provisions for testing equipment, writing area.

3. Create a separate consultation area for customer discussions and demonstrations of contact lens wear and care.

4. Provide for a back-of-the-shop work area for assembling glasses, adjusting frames, stock, etc.

5. Samples of frames are displayed both on walls and in showcases in retail area.

   - Wall displays are illuminated and designed so that the frames are accessible for customer try-ons.

   - Higher-price frames are in showcases.

6. Stools and chairs at counters for the convenience of customers waiting to be helped or trying on frames are also an important part of the integrated design plan for the shop.

   - Provide both full-length and countertop mirrors.

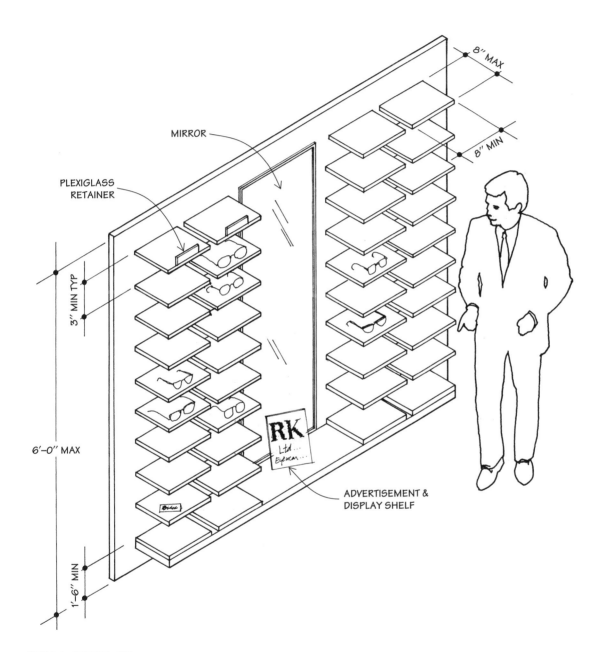

8" MAX

8" MIN

MIRROR

PLEXIGLASS
RETAINER

3" MIN TYP

6'-0" MAX

RK
Ltd...
Eyewear...

ADVERTISEMENT &
DISPLAY SHELF

1'-6" MIN

**WALL DISPLAY**

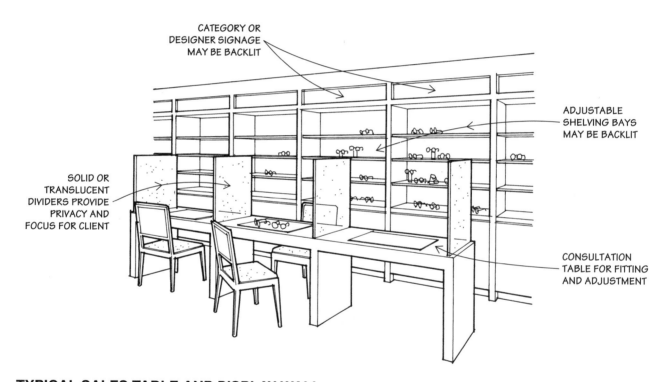

CATEGORY OR
DESIGNER SIGNAGE
MAY BE BACKLIT

ADJUSTABLE
SHELVING BAYS
MAY BE BACKLIT

SOLID OR
TRANSLUCENT
DIVIDERS PROVIDE
PRIVACY AND
FOCUS FOR CLIENT

CONSULTATION
TABLE FOR FITTING
AND ADJUSTMENT

**TYPICAL SALES TABLE AND DISPLAY WALL**

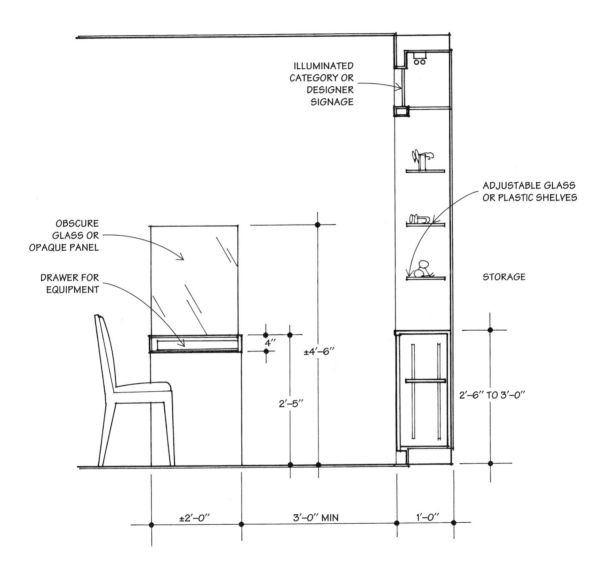

ILLUMINATED
CATEGORY OR
DESIGNER
SIGNAGE

ADJUSTABLE GLASS
OR PLASTIC SHELVES

OBSCURE
GLASS OR
OPAQUE PANEL

DRAWER FOR
EQUIPMENT

STORAGE

4″

±4′–6″

2′–5″

2′–6″ TO 3′–0″

±2′–0″          3′–0″ MIN          1′–0″

**CROSS-SECTION OF SALES TABLE AND
DISPLAY WALL**

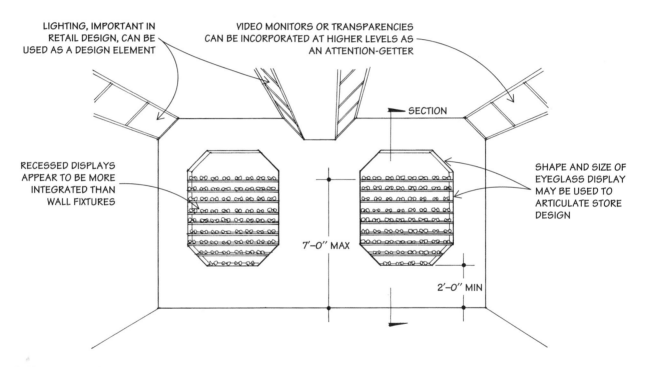

LIGHTING, IMPORTANT IN
RETAIL DESIGN, CAN BE
USED AS A DESIGN ELEMENT

VIDEO MONITORS OR TRANSPARENCIES
CAN BE INCORPORATED AT HIGHER LEVELS AS
AN ATTENTION-GETTER

SECTION

RECESSED DISPLAYS
APPEAR TO BE MORE
INTEGRATED THAN
WALL FIXTURES

SHAPE AND SIZE OF
EYEGLASS DISPLAY
MAY BE USED TO
ARTICULATE STORE
DESIGN

7'-0" MAX

2'-0" MIN

**WALL AND CEILING CONCEPT**

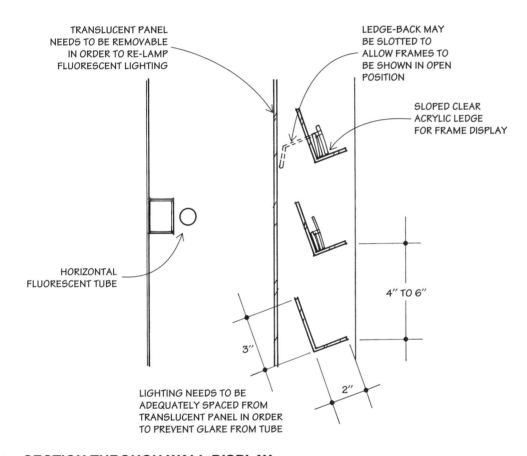

TRANSLUCENT PANEL
NEEDS TO BE REMOVABLE
IN ORDER TO RE-LAMP
FLUORESCENT LIGHTING

LEDGE-BACK MAY
BE SLOTTED TO
ALLOW FRAMES TO
BE SHOWN IN OPEN
POSITION

SLOPED CLEAR
ACRYLIC LEDGE
FOR FRAME DISPLAY

HORIZONTAL
FLUORESCENT TUBE

4" TO 6"

3"

2"

LIGHTING NEEDS TO BE
ADEQUATELY SPACED FROM
TRANSLUCENT PANEL IN ORDER
TO PREVENT GLARE FROM TUBE

## SECTION THROUGH WALL DISPLAY

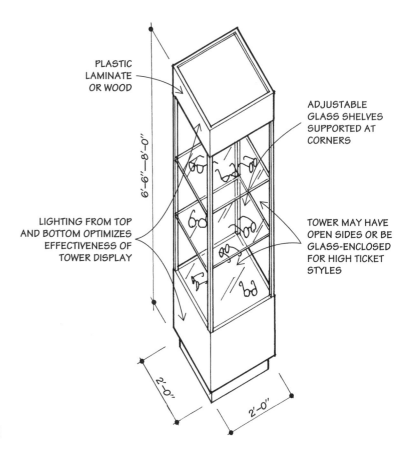

PLASTIC
LAMINATE
OR WOOD

ADJUSTABLE
GLASS SHELVES
SUPPORTED AT
CORNERS

LIGHTING FROM TOP
AND BOTTOM OPTIMIZES
EFFECTIVENESS OF
TOWER DISPLAY

TOWER MAY HAVE
OPEN SIDES OR BE
GLASS-ENCLOSED
FOR HIGH TICKET
STYLES

6'-6"—8'-0"

2'-0"

2'-0"

**GLASS DISPLAY TOWER**

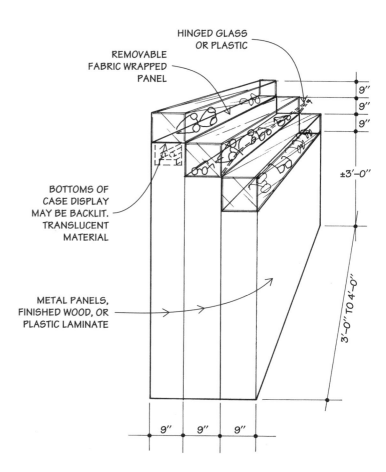

HINGED GLASS
OR PLASTIC

REMOVABLE
FABRIC WRAPPED
PANEL

BOTTOMS OF
CASE DISPLAY
MAY BE BACKLIT.
TRANSLUCENT
MATERIAL

METAL PANELS,
FINISHED WOOD, OR
PLASTIC LAMINATE

9"
9"
9"

±3'-0"

3'-0" TO 4'-0"

9"    9"    9"

**STEPPED FLOOR DISPLAY**

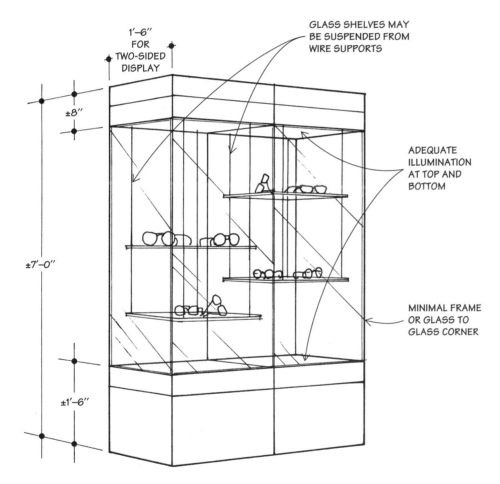

1'-6''
FOR
TWO-SIDED
DISPLAY

±8''

±7'-0''

±1'-6''

GLASS SHELVES MAY
BE SUSPENDED FROM
WIRE SUPPORTS

ADEQUATE
ILLUMINATION
AT TOP AND
BOTTOM

MINIMAL FRAME
OR GLASS TO
GLASS CORNER

**FREE-STANDING OR
WALL CASE**

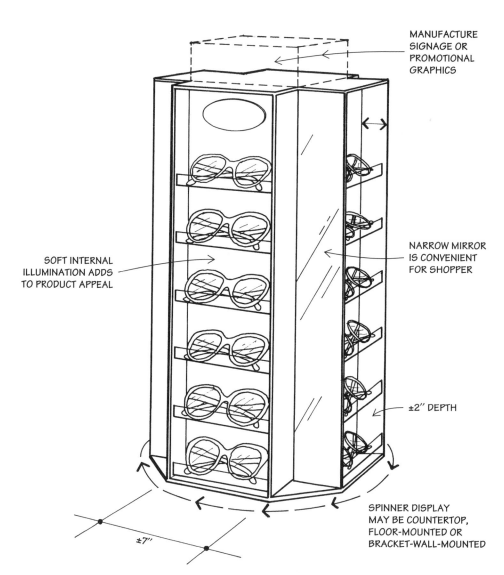

MANUFACTURE
SIGNAGE OR
PROMOTIONAL
GRAPHICS

NARROW MIRROR
IS CONVENIENT
FOR SHOPPER

SOFT INTERNAL
ILLUMINATION ADDS
TO PRODUCT APPEAL

±2" DEPTH

±7"

SPINNER DISPLAY
MAY BE COUNTERTOP,
FLOOR-MOUNTED OR
BRACKET-WALL-MOUNTED

**FOUR-SIDED DISPLAY**

# 18

# Museum Shops

STOCK

OFFICE

BOOKS

AUDIO

CASHWRAP

T-SHIRTS

FEATURE ARCH

**RETAIL STORE
LOCATED OFF THE
MAIN ENTRY OF A
MAJOR MUSEUM**

## Tips and Guidelines

1. Museum shops are a unique store type that brings together the commercial aspects of retailing within an institutional building such as an art museum, library, archive center, or science center.

   ■ Select durable materials with a long life cycle to withstand heavy use generated by high traffic, including groups of students and adults.

2. Museum shops carry many different categories of merchandise, much like the selection found in a specialty mini–department store.

   ■ Many museum shops offer both full-service and self-service merchandising: full-service for high-ticket items such as jewelry, telescopes, binoculars, scarves, and art objects; self-service for impulse and lower-price items, including cards, books, magazines, and tee shirts.

3. Because the customer mix includes both children and adult shoppers, museum shop should be planned to keep merchandise categories separate for these two buying groups.

   ■ Children visiting the institution's shop with school groups buy inexpensive impulse items.

4. Create a traffic pattern and signs that pull customers to the rear of the store.

   ■ Display units should be appropriately sized for ease of selection of books, paper goods, and periodicals.

5. Create three levels of illumination:

   ■ To highlight merchandise within showcases.

   ■ For feature lighting of other merchandise displayed on horizontal surfaces and in wall units.

   ■ Ambient lighting for other areas of the selling floor and support spaces.

6. For functions held after business hours, special merchandise displays should be illuminated, particularly those close to the front of the store or in view through glass partitions.

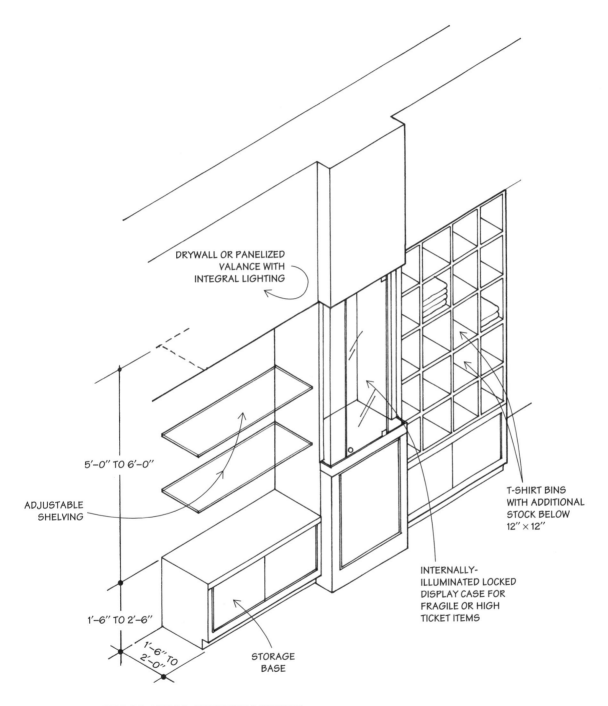

DRYWALL OR PANELIZED
VALANCE WITH
INTEGRAL LIGHTING

5'-0" TO 6'-0"

ADJUSTABLE
SHELVING

1'-6" TO 2'-6"

1'-6" TO
2'-0"

STORAGE
BASE

T-SHIRT BINS
WITH ADDITIONAL
STOCK BELOW
12" × 12"

INTERNALLY-
ILLUMINATED LOCKED
DISPLAY CASE FOR
FRAGILE OR HIGH
TICKET ITEMS

**VIEW OF TYPICAL WALL MERCHANDISE
DISPLAYS**

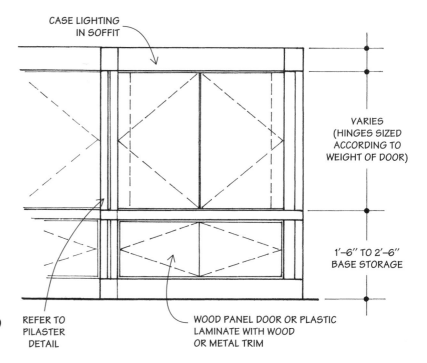

CASE LIGHTING
IN SOFFIT

VARIES
(HINGES SIZED
ACCORDING TO
WEIGHT OF DOOR)

1'–6" TO 2'–6"
BASE STORAGE

**ELEVATION OF PIVOTAL AND
SLIDING DOORS**

REFER TO
PILASTER
DETAIL

WOOD PANEL DOOR OR PLASTIC
LAMINATE WITH WOOD
OR METAL TRIM

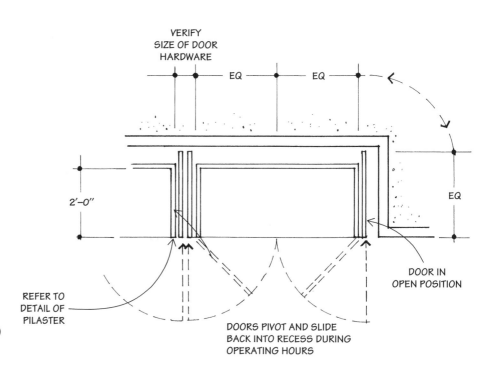

VERIFY
SIZE OF DOOR
HARDWARE

EQ        EQ

EQ

2'–0"

DOOR IN
OPEN POSITION

REFER TO
DETAIL OF
PILASTER

DOORS PIVOT AND SLIDE
BACK INTO RECESS DURING
OPERATING HOURS

**PLAN OF CABINET AND
DOORS**

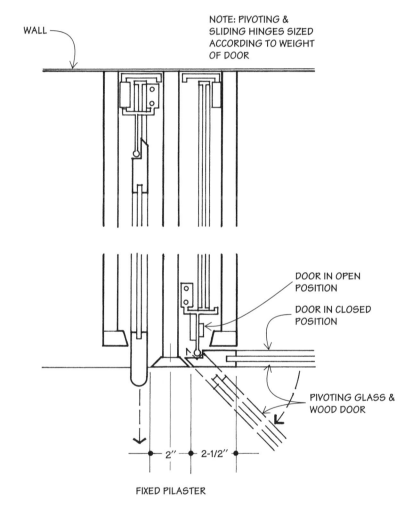

WALL

NOTE: PIVOTING &
SLIDING HINGES SIZED
ACCORDING TO WEIGHT
OF DOOR

DOOR IN OPEN
POSITION

DOOR IN CLOSED
POSITION

PIVOTING GLASS &
WOOD DOOR

2″        2-1/2″

FIXED PILASTER

**PILASTER PLAN DETAIL OF
PIVOTING AND SLIDING GLASS AND
WOOD DOOR IN WALL CABINET**

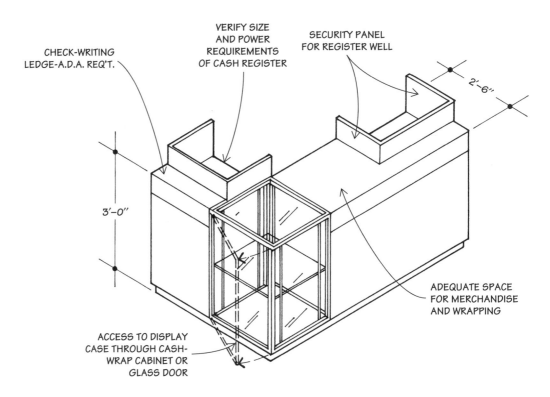

CHECK-WRITING
LEDGE-A.D.A. REQ'T.

VERIFY SIZE
AND POWER
REQUIREMENTS
OF CASH REGISTER

SECURITY PANEL
FOR REGISTER WELL

2'-6"

3'-0"

ACCESS TO DISPLAY
CASE THROUGH CASH-
WRAP CABINET OR
GLASS DOOR

ADEQUATE SPACE
FOR MERCHANDISE
AND WRAPPING

**CORNER GLASS DISPLAY AT CASHWRAP**

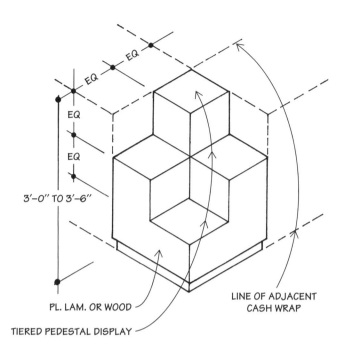

EQ
EQ
EQ
EQ

3'-0" TO 3'-6"

LINE OF ADJACENT
CASH WRAP

PL. LAM. OR WOOD

TIERED PEDESTAL DISPLAY

**CORNER STEP DISPLAY**

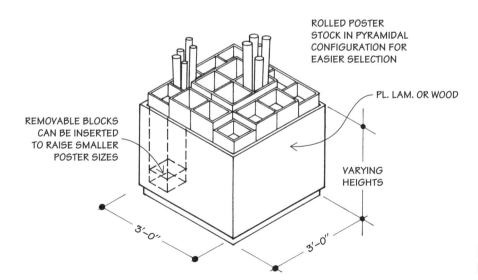

ROLLED POSTER
STOCK IN PYRAMIDAL
CONFIGURATION FOR
EASIER SELECTION

PL. LAM. OR WOOD

REMOVABLE BLOCKS
CAN BE INSERTED
TO RAISE SMALLER
POSTER SIZES

VARYING
HEIGHTS

3'-0"

3'-0"

**POSTERS AND ROLLED
PAPER PRODUCT BIN**

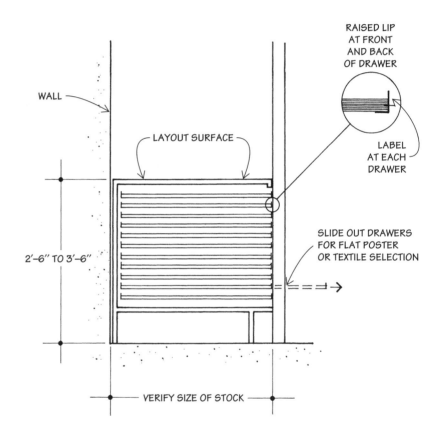

WALL

RAISED LIP
AT FRONT
AND BACK
OF DRAWER

LAYOUT SURFACE

LABEL
AT EACH
DRAWER

2'-6" TO 3'-6"

SLIDE OUT DRAWERS
FOR FLAT POSTER
OR TEXTILE SELECTION

VERIFY SIZE OF STOCK

**SECTION THROUGH FLAT
PULL-OUT POSTER AND PRINT
STORAGE**

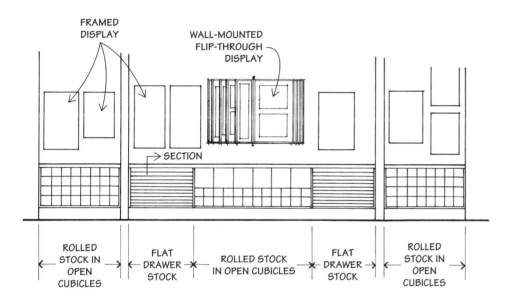

FRAMED
DISPLAY

WALL-MOUNTED
FLIP-THROUGH
DISPLAY

SECTION

ROLLED
STOCK IN
OPEN
CUBICLES

FLAT
DRAWER
STOCK

ROLLED STOCK
IN OPEN CUBICLES

FLAT
DRAWER
STOCK

ROLLED
STOCK IN
OPEN
CUBICLES

**POSTER AND PRINT
DEPARTMENT WALL**

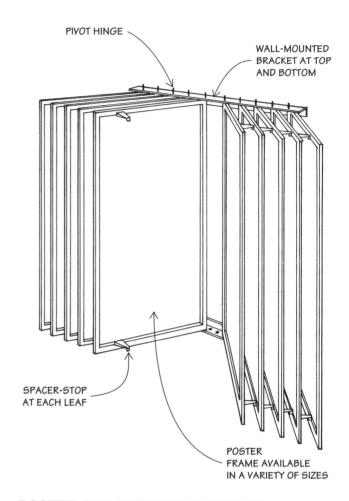

PIVOT HINGE

WALL-MOUNTED
BRACKET AT TOP
AND BOTTOM

SPACER-STOP
AT EACH LEAF

POSTER
FRAME AVAILABLE
IN A VARIETY OF SIZES

**POSTER AND PRINT LEAF DISPLAY**

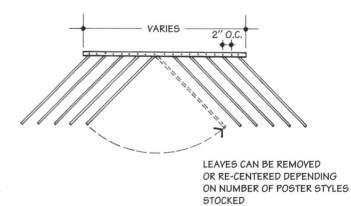

VARIES

2" O.C.

LEAVES CAN BE REMOVED
OR RE-CENTERED DEPENDING
ON NUMBER OF POSTER STYLES
STOCKED

**PLAN OF POSTER AND PRINT DISPLAY**

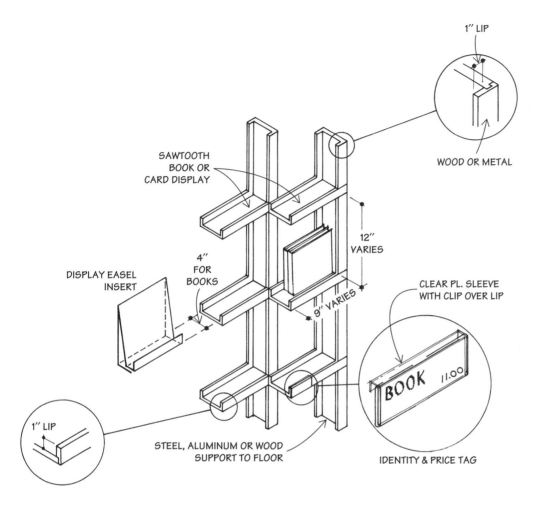

1″ LIP

WOOD OR METAL

SAWTOOTH
BOOK OR
CARD DISPLAY

12″
VARIES

DISPLAY EASEL
INSERT

4″
FOR
BOOKS

9″ VARIES

CLEAR PL. SLEEVE
WITH CLIP OVER LIP

BOOK  11.00

1″ LIP

STEEL, ALUMINUM OR WOOD
SUPPORT TO FLOOR

IDENTITY & PRICE TAG

## OVERLAP BOOK DISPLAY

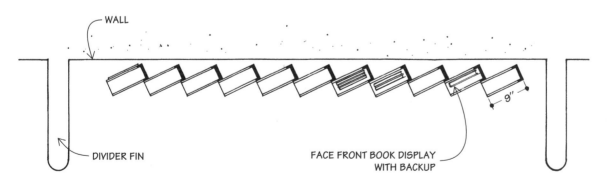

WALL

DIVIDER FIN

FACE FRONT BOOK DISPLAY
WITH BACKUP

9″

## PLAN OF OVERLAP BOOK DISPLAY—
## MODULE

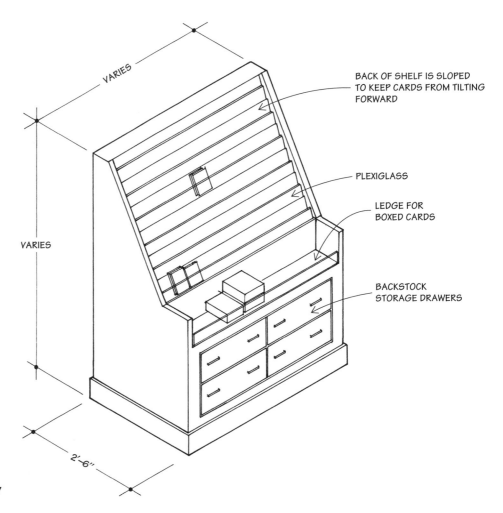

BACK OF SHELF IS SLOPED
TO KEEP CARDS FROM TILTING
FORWARD

PLEXIGLASS

LEDGE FOR
BOXED CARDS

BACKSTOCK
STORAGE DRAWERS

VARIES

VARIES

2'-6"

**CARD DISPLAY**

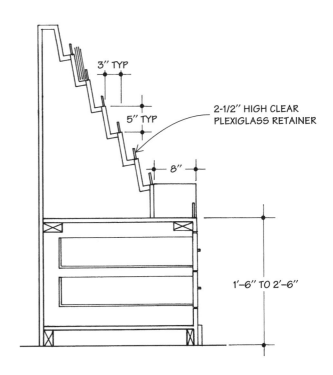

3" TYP

5" TYP

2-1/2" HIGH CLEAR
PLEXIGLASS RETAINER

8"

1'-6" TO 2'-6"

**SECTION THROUGH CARD DISPLAY**

# 19

# Toy Stores

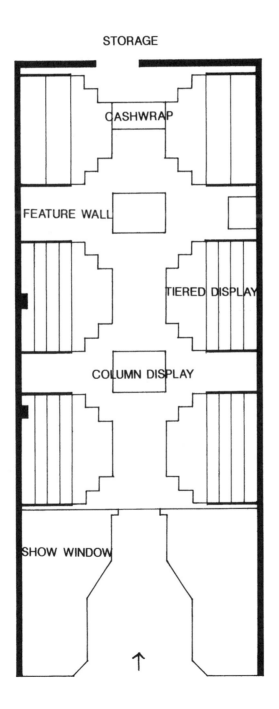

STORAGE

CASHWRAP

FEATURE WALL

TIERED DISPLAY

COLUMN DISPLAY

SHOW WINDOW

**A STREET-LEVEL
ONE-FLOOR SHOP
FOR AN INDEPENDENT
MERCHANT**

## Tips and Guidelines

1. Merchandise assortment includes educational toys and electronic learning machines as well as traditional children's playthings.

   - Outlets range in size from neighborhood shops to megastores.

2. Displays and merchandise presentation should appeal to shoppers of all age groups.

   - Merchandise touch-and-feel plays a major role in influencing buying decisions.

3. Consider crowd control and heavy traffic flow during the peak selling season in November and December when toy stores do more than one-half of their annual business.

4. Wherever possible, create a fun and colorful atmosphere.

   - Allow space for vignettes and demonstration areas.

   - Consider potential hazards: sharp corners, protruding objects, exposed electric outlets, and breakable light fixtures.

5. Toy merchants generate traffic with such special events as celebrity visits, readings, and book signings.

   - A flexible area can be suitable for in-person appearances and similar promotions, and used at other times for product displays.

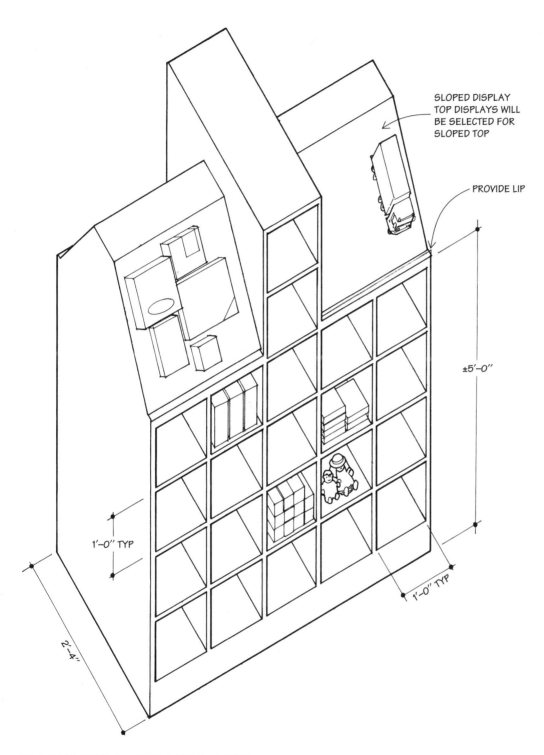

SLOPED DISPLAY
TOP DISPLAYS WILL
BE SELECTED FOR
SLOPED TOP

PROVIDE LIP

±5'–0''

1'–0'' TYP

1'–0'' TYP

2'–4''

## SLOPED TOP SHELF AND NICHES

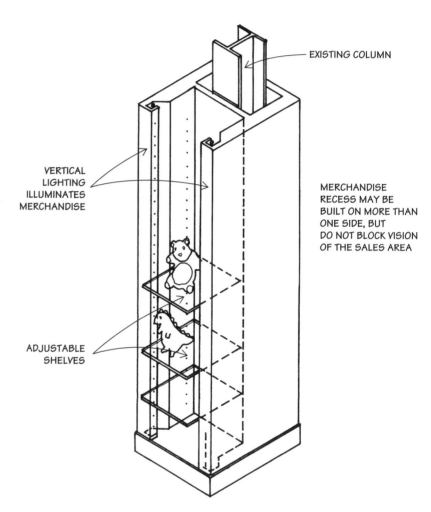

EXISTING COLUMN

VERTICAL
LIGHTING
ILLUMINATES
MERCHANDISE

MERCHANDISE
RECESS MAY BE
BUILT ON MORE THAN
ONE SIDE, BUT
DO NOT BLOCK VISION
OF THE SALES AREA

ADJUSTABLE
SHELVES

**COLUMN DETAIL**

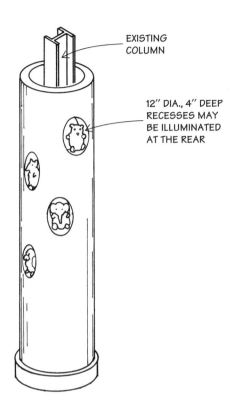

EXISTING
COLUMN

12″ DIA., 4″ DEEP
RECESSES MAY
BE ILLUMINATED
AT THE REAR

**ALTERNATE COLUMN DETAIL**

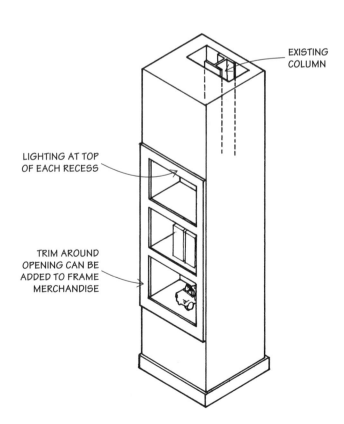

EXISTING
COLUMN

LIGHTING AT TOP
OF EACH RECESS

TRIM AROUND
OPENING CAN BE
ADDED TO FRAME
MERCHANDISE

**ALTERNATE COLUMN DETAIL**

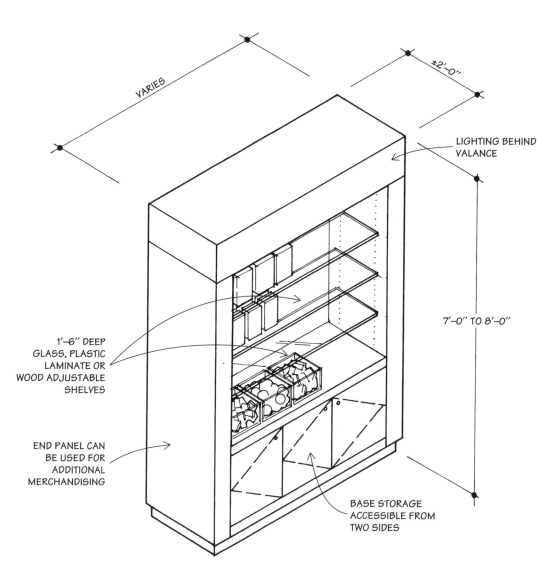

VARIES

±2'-0"

LIGHTING BEHIND
VALANCE

7'-0" TO 8'-0"

1'-6" DEEP
GLASS, PLASTIC
LAMINATE OR
WOOD ADJUSTABLE
SHELVES

END PANEL CAN
BE USED FOR
ADDITIONAL
MERCHANDISING

BASE STORAGE
ACCESSIBLE FROM
TWO SIDES

**TALL CABINET SHELVING**

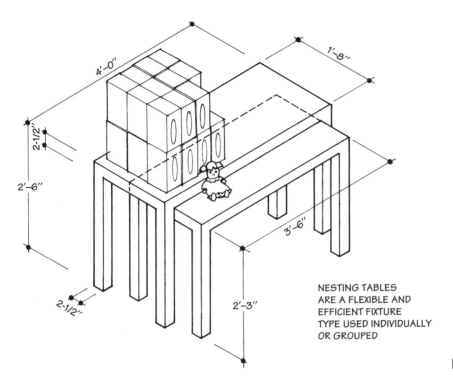

4'-0"

1'-8"

2-1/2"

2'-6"

2-1/2"

3'-6"

2'-3"

NESTING TABLES
ARE A FLEXIBLE AND
EFFICIENT FIXTURE
TYPE USED INDIVIDUALLY
OR GROUPED

## NESTING TABLES

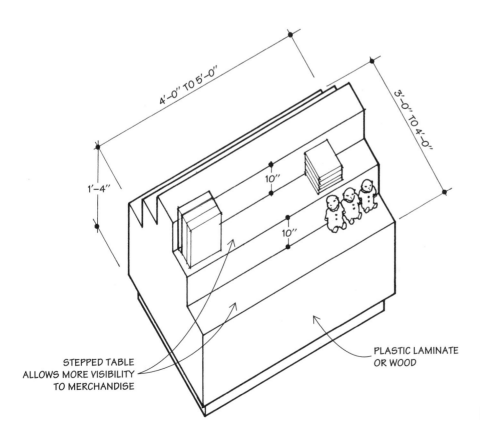

4'-0" TO 5'-0"

3'-0" TO 4'-0"

1'-4"

10"

10"

STEPPED TABLE
ALLOWS MORE VISIBILITY
TO MERCHANDISE

PLASTIC LAMINATE
OR WOOD

## STEPPED TABLE

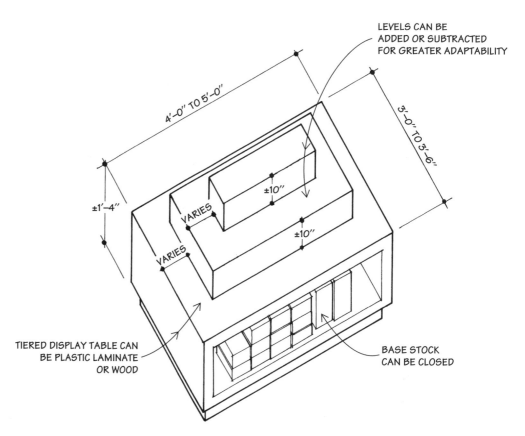

LEVELS CAN BE
ADDED OR SUBTRACTED
FOR GREATER ADAPTABILITY

4'-0" TO 5'-0"

3'-0" TO 3'-6"

±1'-4"

±10"

±10"

VARIES

VARIES

TIERED DISPLAY TABLE CAN
BE PLASTIC LAMINATE
OR WOOD

BASE STOCK
CAN BE CLOSED

**STEP-TIER DISPLAY FOR TOYS, BOXED
ITEMS**

# 20

# Hardware Stores

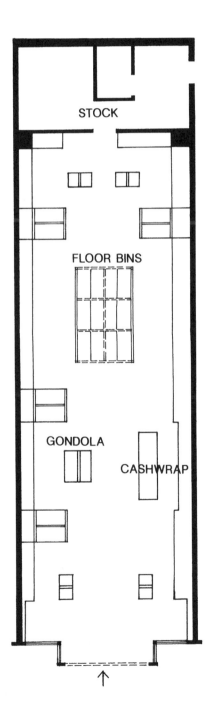

STOCK

FLOOR BINS

GONDOLA

CASHWRAP

**SINGLE-LEVEL
HARDWARE STORE IN
A SHOPPING MALL**

## Tips and Guidelines

1. Types of stores in this category include independent neighborhood shops, chain stores, megamarts, and contractor's supply operations.

2. Product selection and distribution procedures determine layout of shopping area.

   ▪ Aisle width can range from the typical three feet up to eight feet, which is wide enough to accommodate a small fork-lift truck.

3. Sign program should be included early in the planning of the store's design.

   ▪ Hanging signs and banners direct customers around the selling area.

   ▪ Signs at displays give specifications, benefits, installation requirements, price.

4. For home improvement stores where customers require assistance to plan such spaces as kitchens and bathrooms, an enclosed conference or sit-down area is useful for holding product and installation discussions.

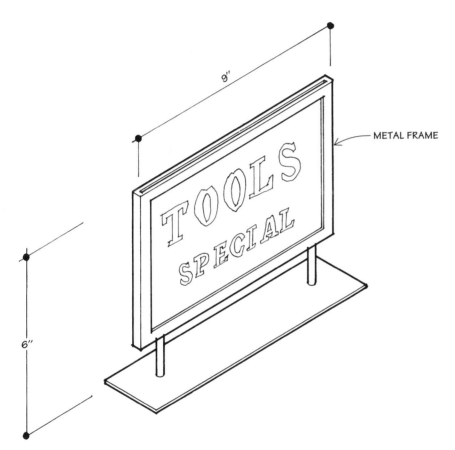

9"

METAL FRAME

6"

**SIGN STAND**

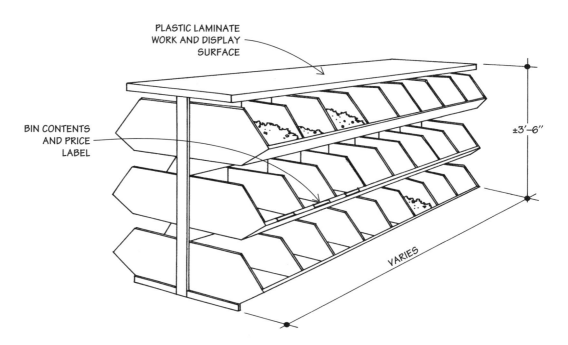

PLASTIC LAMINATE
WORK AND DISPLAY
SURFACE

BIN CONTENTS
AND PRICE
LABEL

±3'–6"

VARIES

**BULK FLOOR UNIT**

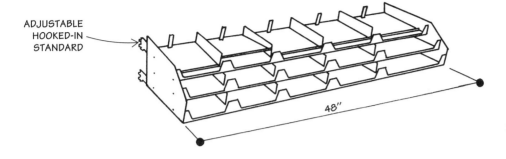

ADJUSTABLE
HOOKED-IN
STANDARD

48"

**SANDPAPER DISPLAY
UNIT**

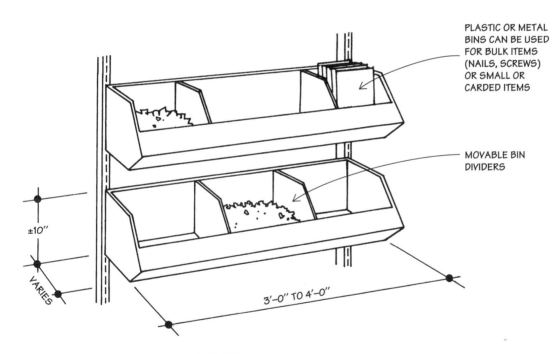

PLASTIC OR METAL
BINS CAN BE USED
FOR BULK ITEMS
(NAILS, SCREWS)
OR SMALL OR
CARDED ITEMS

MOVABLE BIN
DIVIDERS

±10"

VARIES

3'-0" TO 4'-0"

**BULK WALL OR GONDOLA BINS**

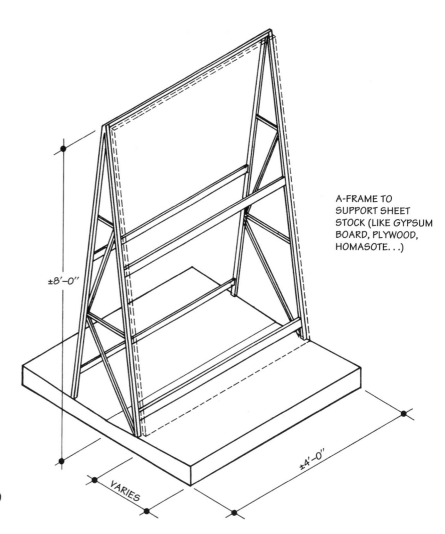

A-FRAME TO
SUPPORT SHEET
STOCK (LIKE GYPSUM
BOARD, PLYWOOD,
HOMASOTE. . .)

±8'–0"

±4'–0"

VARIES

**A-FRAME STAND FOR BOARD
MERCHANDISE**

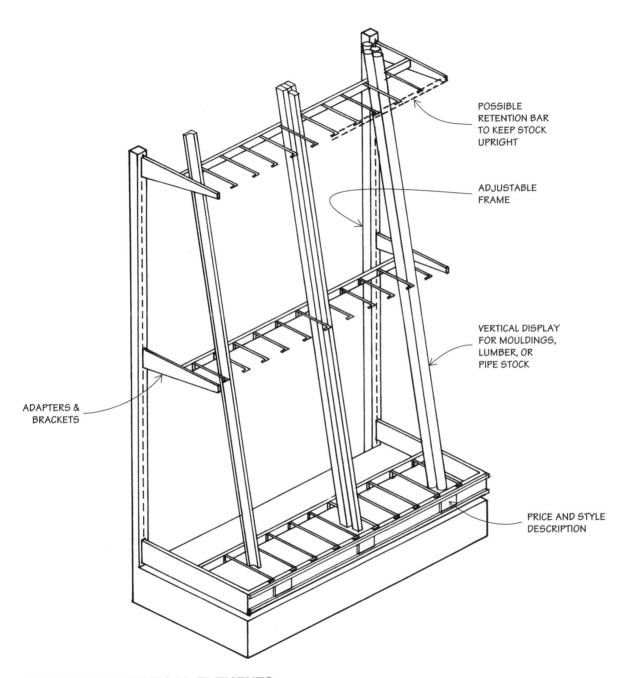

POSSIBLE
RETENTION BAR
TO KEEP STOCK
UPRIGHT

ADJUSTABLE
FRAME

VERTICAL DISPLAY
FOR MOULDINGS,
LUMBER, OR
PIPE STOCK

ADAPTERS &
BRACKETS

PRICE AND STYLE
DESCRIPTION

## DISPLAY FOR VERTICAL ELEMENTS

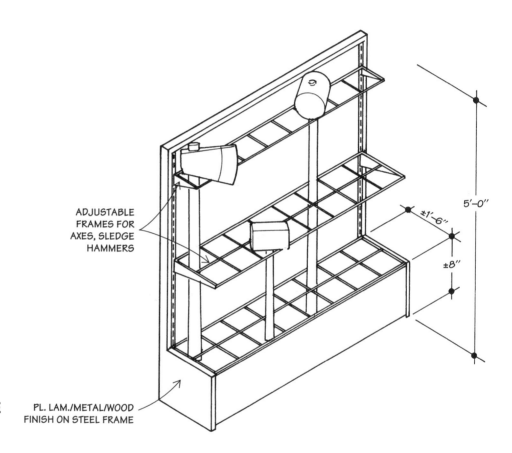

ADJUSTABLE
FRAMES FOR
AXES, SLEDGE
HAMMERS

5'-0"

±1'-6"

±8"

**LONG-HANDLE
DISPLAY UNIT**

PL. LAM./METAL/WOOD
FINISH ON STEEL FRAME

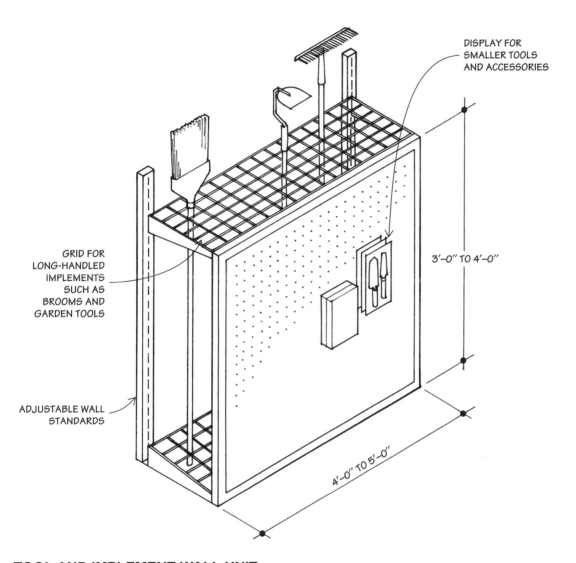

DISPLAY FOR
SMALLER TOOLS
AND ACCESSORIES

GRID FOR
LONG-HANDLED
IMPLEMENTS
SUCH AS
BROOMS AND
GARDEN TOOLS

3'–0" TO 4'–0"

ADJUSTABLE WALL
STANDARDS

4'–0" TO 5'–0"

**TOOL AND IMPLEMENT WALL UNIT**

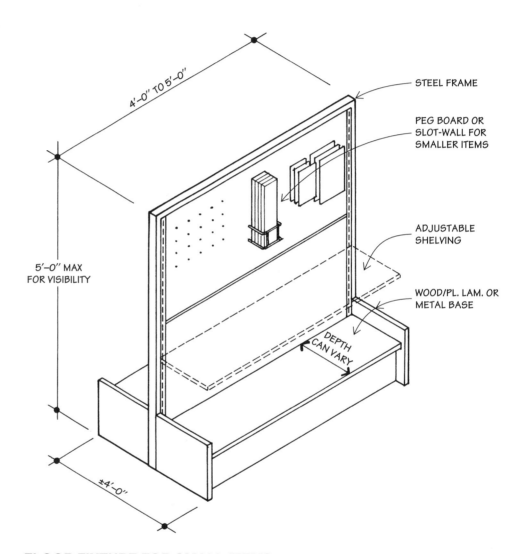

4'-0" TO 5'-0"

STEEL FRAME

PEG BOARD OR
SLOT-WALL FOR
SMALLER ITEMS

ADJUSTABLE
SHELVING

5'-0" MAX
FOR VISIBILITY

WOOD/PL. LAM. OR
METAL BASE

DEPTH
CAN VARY

±4'-0"

**FLOOR FIXTURE FOR SMALL ITEMS**

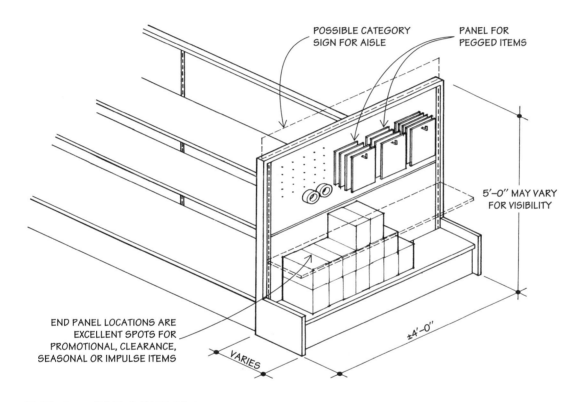

POSSIBLE CATEGORY
SIGN FOR AISLE

PANEL FOR
PEGGED ITEMS

5'–0" MAY VARY
FOR VISIBILITY

±4'–0"

VARIES

END PANEL LOCATIONS ARE
EXCELLENT SPOTS FOR
PROMOTIONAL, CLEARANCE,
SEASONAL OR IMPULSE ITEMS

**END-CAP FOR GONDOLA**

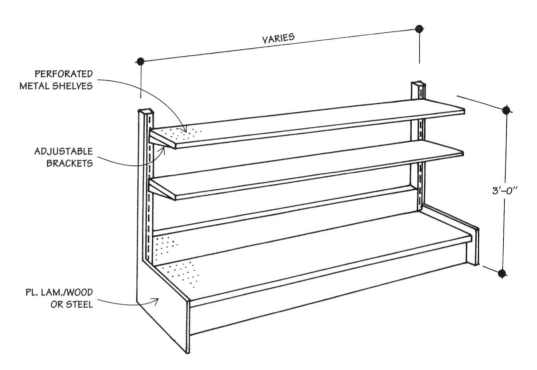

**ADJUSTABLE SHELVING UNIT FOR HEAVY PRODUCTS**

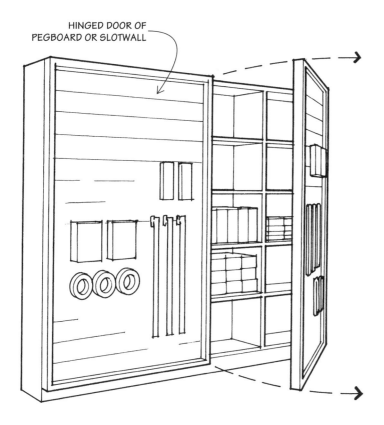

HINGED DOOR OF
PEGBOARD OR SLOTWALL

**WALL DISPLAY WITH BACK STORAGE**

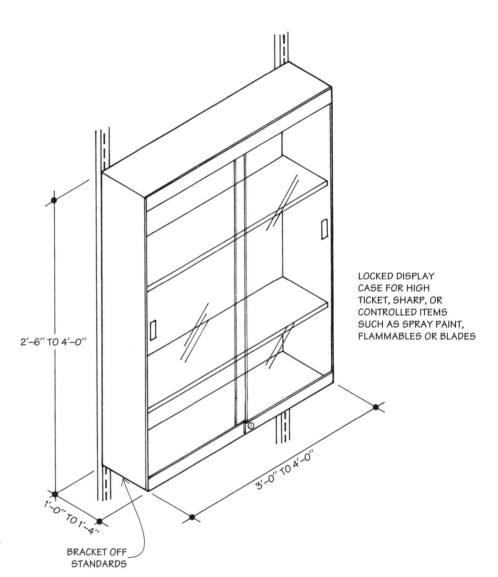

2′–6″ TO 4′–0″

1′–0″ TO 1′–4″

3′–0″ TO 4′–0″

LOCKED DISPLAY
CASE FOR HIGH
TICKET, SHARP, OR
CONTROLLED ITEMS
SUCH AS SPRAY PAINT,
FLAMMABLES OR BLADES

**GLASS WALL DISPLAY
CASE**

BRACKET OFF
STANDARDS

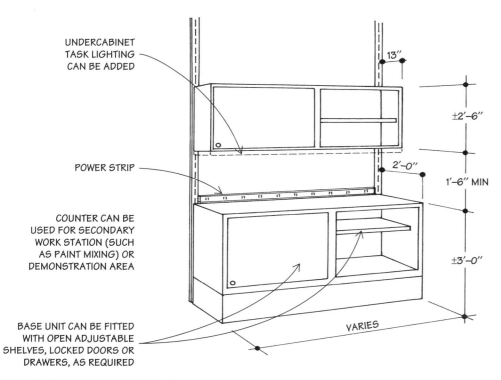

UNDERCABINET
TASK LIGHTING
CAN BE ADDED

13"

±2'-6"

POWER STRIP

2'-0"

1'-6" MIN

COUNTER CAN BE
USED FOR SECONDARY
WORK STATION (SUCH
AS PAINT MIXING) OR
DEMONSTRATION AREA

±3'-0"

BASE UNIT CAN BE FITTED
WITH OPEN ADJUSTABLE
SHELVES, LOCKED DOORS OR
DRAWERS, AS REQUIRED

VARIES

**MULTIPURPOSE BASE AND
CABINET UNIT**

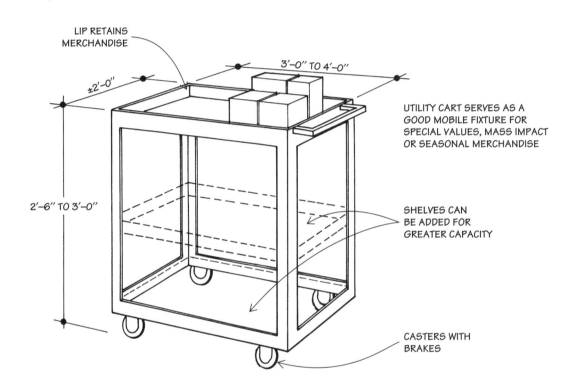

LIP RETAINS
MERCHANDISE

±2'-0"

3'-0" TO 4'-0"

UTILITY CART SERVES AS A
GOOD MOBILE FIXTURE FOR
SPECIAL VALUES, MASS IMPACT
OR SEASONAL MERCHANDISE

2'-6" TO 3'-0"

SHELVES CAN
BE ADDED FOR
GREATER CAPACITY

CASTERS WITH
BRAKES

**ROLLING CART**

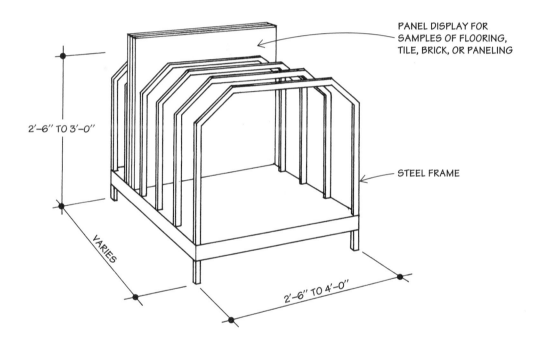

PANEL DISPLAY FOR
SAMPLES OF FLOORING,
TILE, BRICK, OR PANELING

STEEL FRAME

2'–6'' TO 3'–0''

VARIES

2'–6'' TO 4'–0''

**PANEL DISPLAY UNIT**

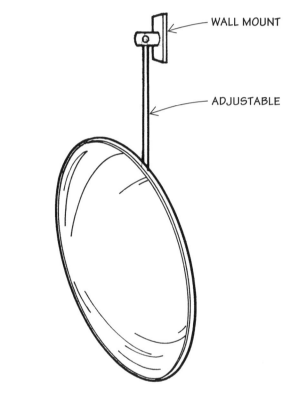

WALL MOUNT

ADJUSTABLE

**SECURITY MIRROR**

# Index

## ABOUT THE AUTHORS

CHARLES E. BROUDY, FAIA, is president and principal of Charles E. Broudy & Associates, P.C., an architectural and planning firm based in Philadelphia that specializes in retail store design. Mr. Broudy's firm has designed over 4000 retail stores in the United States and overseas. His clients include The Gap, Ann Taylor, PetroCanada, and the John F. Kennedy Library Shop. A graduate of Drexel University and a past president of the Philadelphia Chapter of the American Institute of Architects, Mr. Broudy is a frequent lecturer on trends in store planning and design to trade and professional groups.

VILMA BARR, coauthor with Charles E. Broudy of *Designing to Sell*, is an editorial and promotion consultant based in New York City. Her work appears in the design and business press on topics related to communications and marketing. She received her B.S. from Drexel University and attended the Massachusetts Institute of Technology for graduate studies. Ms. Barr, author of *The Best of Neon* and *The Illustrated Room: Interior Rendering in the 20th Century*, is a press member of the American Society of Interior Designers and an affiliate member of the American Institute of Architects.